"The Runner"

Pat Ward

DEDICATION

This book is dedicated to my brother Val,
my hero.

"The Runner"

Title: "The Runner"
ISBN: 9798876854063

Copyright © 2023 Pat Ward

All rights reserved. This book or any portion thereof may not be reproduced or used in any manner whatsoever without the express written permission of the author except for the use of brief quotations in a book review.

Cover based on an original sketch by John Rabbitt
Stylised by Bahar Turan

Printed and published by Pat Ward
First printing: 2024

Author: Pat Ward

Email: therunner1947@gmail.com

Paperback copies and ebook copies available at www.therunner.ie and all amazon webstores.

Paperback copies also available at Charlie Byrne Bookstore at Middle Street, Galway, Ireland, and from their website:
www.charliebyrne.ie/product/the-runner

"The Runner"

Contents		**Page**
Introduction		4
Chapter 1	Patsy Ward	6
Chapter 2	A New Life In England	49
Chapter 3	Return To Ireland	92
Chapter 4	The Gift Of Family & Friends	163

"The Runner"

Introduction

My name is Pat Ward. I have been asked on numerous occasions to write a story about my life but I held off doing so mainly because of a dread of revisiting my childhood. The initial requests for the book came from my siblings, but they understood and accepted my reasons for not taking on that project. As the years went by the requests came from friends who felt that the book might serve as an inspiration to others, but I still resisted their entreaties. I also baulked at the notion of writing a book with a title like "Pat Ward – My Story", or any other title with a direct reference to myself.

In February of 2023 I reached a new milestone in my life when I retired, and although it would give me the time to write the book, I was still reluctant to do so. In April 2023 John Rabbitt and I met up for a coffee. John was one of my regular golfing 4 ball partners, and he asked me how my retirement was going. He then brought up the topic of writing a book about my life, but this time he suggested a title. John explained that during our numerous rounds of golf I had told stories or talked about events in my life that he and our friends had found interesting. John surprised me when he showed me a sketch he had drawn based on one of my stories. He titled the sketch "The Runner". (The significance of the sketch will be explained later). John said that he thought "The Runner" would be a good title for a book about my life and the more I reflected on it the more I warmed to the idea. I felt comfortable with John's proposed title, but I was still reluctant to write the book.

About that same time my only remaining brother Val became seriously ill with cancer, and having retired I had more time to visit Val in England. In the course of those visits and our phone conversations the issue of a book arose again. I told Val about the title suggested by John and he said it would be a great title. I finally decided to write the book and I gave it the title

"The Runner"

"The Runner", as suggested by John. His sketch was transformed by a student named Bahar Turan into the image used for the front and back covers of the book.

Chapter 1 deals with my childhood and I struggled to write that chapter because it forced me to address a childhood that I had elected to forget, but the book couldn't have been written without revisiting that era in my life. I owed it to myself and to my family to do so, but I also owed it to the many thousands of boys who were placed in institutions, the so called "Industrial Schools".

Whilst Chapter 1 may make for some depressing reading it is not meant to be a litany of complaints about my childhood, but it should rather be seen as the base from which I had to start out in life. I now look back on my childhood as the platform upon which my character was built and which determined the outcome of my subsequent life. We all have to start from somewhere, and that was my launchpad. Hopefully the subsequent chapters will be more uplifting.

"The Runner"

Chapter 1 – Patsy Ward

The Irish famine lasted for several years in the 1840's. More than one million people died of starvation and millions were left impoverished and destitute. The British rulers decided to build "Workhouses" (also known as "Poorhouses") to house people and provide food and shelter because people could no longer live off the land. The workhouses were so called because in exchange for food and shelter the inhabitants were made to work for free. About 130 such poorhouses were built in the 1840's and the 1850's and they housed about 300,000 people. Due to the limited capacity many thousands of people were denied access. Many of those starved to death. Many emigrated. My great grandparents were amongst the lucky ones who survived the famine.

The famine ended around 1847, but by then poverty was endemic and entrenched in Ireland and would last well into the 20th century. The poorhouses would continue to play a vital role in Ireland up to the 1920's. My grandmother was an inmate in a poorhouse in Galway and she gave birth to my mother there in 1910.

The workhouse in Galway was demolished in 1920 and became the site of University College Hospital Galway (UCHG). My mother and the remaining inmates were transferred to a workhouse in Loughrea.

I never knew my grandmother, but I can only assume that she had a very difficult life. It would transpire that my mother would also have a very difficult life.

My mother had six children, Dennis - born in 1939, Margaret (Pearl) - 1941, Ethel - 1943, Valentine (Val)- 1945, Patrick (me) - 1947, and Anthony - 1949. I was always called Patsy by the family, a name that is commonly used for boys in Ireland. In 1950 my mother found herself abandoned with six children. There was no

"The Runner"

State support system for single or deserted mothers in Ireland in those days, but the State had another solution, and that was simply to take the children from such mothers and place them in institutions. Convents and Industrial Schools were used for that purpose. Val and I were sent to Letterfrack Christian Brothers School (CBS), near Clifden, Galway. Dennis was sent to St Joseph's CBS in Salthill, Galway. Pearl and Ethel were sent to St Anne's Industrial School, Galway, (known locally as "The Lenaboy").
My mother and Anthony were taken in by a Mr and Mrs Commins in Galway, with State support payments.

Letterfrack is the name of a village located near Clifden in County Galway on the west coast of Ireland, and the western region of Co. Galway is known as Connemara which is a derivation of the Irish name *Conmhaícne Mara*. The Conmhaícne were an early Irish tribe who gave their name to that region. The word '*Mara*' is derived from the Irish word for the sea 'muir'.

Letterfrack is an anglicisation of the Irish name, *Leitir Fraic*. *Leitir* refers to a waterlogged hillside. The origin of *Fraic* is unknown, but it is thought to have been a distortion of the Irish word *Bhreac*, (pronounced "vrack"), a speckled wet hillside.
So, we have a waterlogged hillside and a speckled wet hillside on the western seaboard which together describe a bleak foreboding place where the weather was more often than not wild, wet and windy.

Letterfrack was a living nightmare for me. I was three years old surrounded by boys aged up to 16 years old. I clung constantly to Val even though he was only five years old. He was my protector, my only family, my only friend. The Christian Brothers wore black cassocks, and they looked like fearsome giants to me. I had good cause to be petrified of them because they doled out gratuitous beatings as they thought fit, and they often resorted to punching

"The Runner"

boys with their fists or kicking boys on the ground and beating them with a leather strap. It would not be an understatement to say that Letterfrack was Dickensian in so many ways.

On a dark wet miserable morning in September 1954, Val and I and about 20 other boys were shepherded on to an army truck. We didn't know why, or where we were about to be taken. Later that morning we were off loaded at St. Joseph's Christian Brothers School in Salthill, Galway.

It seems strange to me even now, but from the moment that I alighted from that truck my mind went blank about my time in Letterfrack. It's as if I realised that I would not be going back there, and my mind brought down a protective shutter to forevermore shield me from my experiences there.

Letterfrack has left an indelible mark on my psyche. I cannot go near the place without suffering from a stomach-churning feeling of nausea. Val and I never talked about Letterfrack throughout the rest of our lives. I was in Letterfrack for four years and I have shut my mind completely to my experiences there. They are entombed in the boglands of my mind where they will stay forever. The only reason that I occasionally found myself near the place is because I had been asked by visiting family or friends to take them to Kylemore Abbey and to Clifden and unfortunately I had to drive through Letterfrack to get from one to the other.

St. Joseph's school was located along the sea front in Salthill, and the first thing I noticed was the smell of the seaweed when we got out of the truck. Val was nine years old, and I was seven – still a tiny waif.

The following days, weeks and months would take me on an emotional roller coaster ride where I would experience happiness, sadness, and utter confusion in my new world. Moving from Letterfrack to St. Joseph's was like moving from never ending

"The Runner"

darkness to light. I had shut myself down in Letterfrack and to all intents I was a dormant person. But in St Joseph's I started to see light in a way that I had never seen it before. Compared to Letterfrack, St Joseph's had a brightness and an airiness about the place that invited me to emerge from my mental cave. However, St. Joseph's too would soon reveal its demons.

On that first morning in St Joseph's we were taken to a hall where the Brothers went through an administrative process of checking our names and giving us numbers to identify our clothes. My number was 115 and Val's was 196 and our clothes would have a patch with our number stitched into them. We still wore boots and short trousers, and it would be a long time before we would start to wear shoes, long trousers or underpants.

When the administration work was done we were taken to the main yard where the resident boys were playing. I was to discover later that there were about 150 boys in total at St. Joseph's. I was still very shy and very insecure, and I clung to Val because I was afraid that I would be beaten by the bigger boys who were very boisterous and noisy. Val took me over to see a big boy in the yard. He smiled at me and said, "Hello Patsy. I'm your brother Dennis." He then grabbed me and raised me above his head. I thought he was going to throw me to the ground, and I screamed with fear. Dennis laughed and put me down gently and said: "Don't you recognise me? I'm your brother Dennis."

I didn't recognise him, but I had a vague recollection of what Ethel and Pearl looked like and he looked a bit like them, so I assumed that he really was Dennis. Val had spoken about him many times, and finally he was here in front of me. Dennis held me close and said:

"Don't be afraid. I'll look after you and if any big boy goes near you just let me know and I'll smash his face."

"The Runner"

I had never heard language like that before and I was wondering if Dennis had turned into a bully, but he was just being protective. I was pale and puny in contrast to Dennis who was tanned and muscular. Dennis went off to play with the big boys, and Val and I started to mix with the smaller boys.

Sadly, Dennis reached the age of 16 within a few months of my arrival, and suddenly he was gone. It was standard practice to get the boys out of the school when they reached the age of 16. This was achieved by placing them with a family as cheap labour, more often than not with a farming family. I was soon to discover that Dennis had been placed with a farming family in Tuam, Co. Galway.

One Sunday morning several weeks after leaving the school Dennis turned up to visit Val and me. He shocked us when he said he was taking us on a bicycle to the farm in Tuam. He mounted the bike, pulled Val up to sit on the carrier at the back of the bike and then lifted me up on to the crossbar and off he went peddling the bike to Tuam. That is a distance of about 25 miles, and he was just 16 years old!! He was powerful for his age. I could feel his warm breath on my neck as he used all of his strength to get that bicycle up several hills, but he did it. The farmer's wife gave us dinner which was followed by apple pie. I saw what I thought were some tea leaves in the apple pie, but when I bit into them they tasted awful. That was my first encounter with cloves.

During our time there the farmer put Dennis to work on the farm and we hardly saw him. Finally, he too had dinner and some apple pie, and then took us back to the school on the bike. Dennis must have clocked up over 100 miles of cycling that day.

I can still sense Dennis' warm breath on the back of my neck some seventy years later, a warm reassuring breath. I never doubted for a moment that Dennis would get us to Tuam and back to Galway.

"The Runner"

A few months later Val received a letter from Dennis saying that he had emigrated to England. I think the reason for him taking us on that trip to Tuam was because Dennis wanted to see us before he headed to England. That was the last I was to see of my big brother Dennis for another nine years.

Shortly after the Tuam trip a Brother took Val and me to a room at the front of the school and in the room stood a small woman. She immediately rushed over and grabbed us, hugging us closely and repeating our names mantra like, "Val, Val, little Patsy, so tiny." The hugging seemed to last for ages and as kisses started to be showered on us I became hugely embarrassed. The kisses stopped momentarily and suddenly I started to feel water fall on my face, and when I looked up I saw a stream of tears flowing from my mother's eyes. She smothered us in more kisses which left me blushing profusely. I didn't know what to do with my hands, but any chance of reciprocating those hugs had been beaten out of me in Letterfrack where any kind of affection was punishable with the strap or a slap in the face. I felt safe with my mother and I wanted to stay with her, but that was not to be. In time I would come to realise that her emotional outpouring had been an expression of unconditional love, something I would recall with joy when I thought about that feeling, and with sadness at its absence.

The Brother stayed in the room throughout the visit watching carefully like a prison guard. He didn't give the slightest hint that he had in any way been affected by that reunion.

The visit ended much too soon and as she kissed us goodbye my mother said:

"Don't worry my darlings, I will get you out of here and we will be a family again."

"The Runner"

My mother left the room first, and as Val and I were led back to the yard I found myself in a total state of confusion because I couldn't understand why we weren't going home with her. I asked Val to explain that, but he couldn't. That was the first time I saw him bite his lip, and that was to become his life-long sign that he was suppressing his emotions. I on the other hand could not suppress mine and I simply cried.

By now my life seemed to comprise a series of shocks and surprises with the move from Letterfrack to St. Joseph's, meeting and losing Dennis within a few months and meeting my mother. But there were more surprises in store.

One Sunday Val and I were taken to the Lenaboy in Galway to be reintroduced to our sisters, Ethel and Pearl. It seems that someone somewhere was working at reconnecting the family again. When we arrived at the Lenaboy we were taken by a nun to a play area and introduced to Pearl and Ethel. Pearl was 13 years old; Ethel was 11, Val was nine and I was seven.

Pearl and Val were animated and excited at meeting up again and went racing off to play on some swings. Ethel and I were both terribly shy, and we sat on opposite ends of a bench. We introduced social distancing to the world that day.

Neither of us spoke, and we both simply stared down at the ground. Ethel was in a white dress and wore shiny black shoes and white ankle socks. I think the nuns had dressed her up specially for the occasion. I was in drab clothes with short pants and scruffy boots and non-descript socks. We both stared at the ground and after what seemed like an eternity Ethel started swinging her legs back and forth and her white socks caught my eye. I decided to swing my legs back and forth to synchronise with hers, but then she stopped suddenly, and my legs were momentarily left floating all alone in mid-air. I then stopped swinging my legs. She turned her head to the side as if to listen to the grass with her left ear,

"The Runner"

but she was in fact taking a sly peek at me. I looked to my right with embarrassment. We then went back to staring at the ground again.

We never said a word to each other, but in our silence we bonded that day. That bond would solidify and grow in strength over the coming years and to this day I don't know why, but I simply felt a comfort in her company.

Dennis had previously told us that we had a younger brother named Anthony, and Pearl mentioned that he also lived in Galway and that we would meet him soon.

As time passed by I became more and more puzzled as to why our mother didn't come back to visit us again, but Val couldn't explain it. Then one Sunday Val and I were taken to meet Anthony. He was living with Mr and Mrs Commins and their two grown up daughters in St Brendan's Terrace, Galway, but my mother was nowhere to be seen. I asked about my mother, and I was told that she was away!! Anthony was excited to discover two of his long-lost brothers and he and Val went off to play while I, still suffering from chronic shyness, just sat by the turf fire. I was sad that my mother was not there, and I didn't feel secure with the Commins family who were total strangers to me.

The situation as I could then comprehend it in early 1955 was that Val and I were in St Joseph's, Ethel and Pearl were at the Lenaboy, Dennis was at a farm in Tuam and Anthony was living with Mr and Mrs Commins, and my mother was "away" - whatever that meant. Within a matter of months Dennis would emigrate to England.

Despite being at St Joseph's for almost a year now, I was still scared of everyone and everything. I was eight years old and I was fine with other boys around my age, but 14- or 15-years old boys were so much bigger and they petrified me. Whenever a group of big boys in hob nailed boots came charging through our group of small boys we faced the choice of being brushed aside or being

"The Runner"

trampled on. Scattering was the only safe option. I missed Dennis not least for his affection for me, but for the protection he gave me. With Dennis gone I was fair game for unfettered bullies, and Val was too small to provide the kind of protection that Dennis had provided. I was riddled with insecurity coupled with a terrible sense of being inferior and inept, and I just continued to stay shut down and keep to myself as much as possible. I envied other boys of my age who were more outgoing, but fear was my constant companion.

Over the following year or so most of the bigger boys had left me alone, but one boy turned out to be a persistent bully and there seemed to be no prospect of escaping from his orbit. There were times when he would deliberately target me and push me to the ground or taunt me to prove his power over me. This went on for months, and so far I had just put up with it, but this timid mouse was about to roar.

Queuing was a common practice in the school, and more often than not the big boys would be at the front of the queue and the smaller boys at the back. One day we were all standing in a queue, and I was near the back. I spotted the bully near the front of the queue, laughing and joking with his friends. We all wore short trousers and hob nailed boots, and I could see the white of his bare legs. An idea suddenly sprang into my mind, ebbing and flowing in equal measure with opportunity and fear. Could I do this? I said to my friends, "I'm going to get that bully", and I started to move up along the queue. Other boys started to push me back, but I raised my finger to my lips to hush them as I pointed towards the bully. They realised that I intended to attack him and allowed me to move forward. I had to make similar pleas several times, but I finally came to within a few feet of the bully. He had his back to me, and I knew that I just had to seize this opportunity. I stared intently at his bare white leg, and I moved up to within inches of him. I cocked my right leg backward and then flung it forward with all my might. My boot was propelled into his

"The Runner"

leg like a cannonball, and I was shocked when he fell to the ground like a sack of potatoes. He was screaming in pain, but I screamed even louder.
"Don't you ever hit me again."

With that I raced back to my place in the queue. The other boys had been watching intently to see how events would unfold and they were delighted when the bully was felled by the timid mouse. I was petrified with fear because I felt that the bully would come after me sooner or later, but he never did. I learned two powerful lessons that day - I could overcome my fear of bullies, and they will back down if you stand up to them.

Prayers
Mass was held in the school chapel every morning at 7.00am after which we had breakfast and then went to school classes. I eventually joined the school choir and learned to sing Latin hymns but I didn't understand a word of Latin. A prayer was said before and after each meal, before the start of the morning class and again before the start of the afternoon class. We said the Angelus at 12.00 noon and again at 6.00pm. The prayers were intended to instil Christian values into us, but we would soon see the hypocrisy of Brothers who mouthed the prayers and behaved in a barbaric or evil manner that instilled fear instead.

Classes
There were six classrooms and I had started in the first class. The first two classes were taught by lay teachers who went home every afternoon after school. They were teaching the youngest boys and showed great patience and tolerance. The remaining classes were run by Brothers, and tough times lay ahead in some of those classes. We were taught Irish, English and Maths, and in the higher classes we were taught Irish history. During my time at St. Joseph's, I would develop a life-long love of poetry which

would allow my imagination to go on journeys into other worlds and provide a temporary escape from my world.

Trades
The institutions into which boys were being placed by the State were known as Industrial Schools with the notion that boys could learn a useful trade there, but that was not really the case. What they had was self-sufficiency. St Joseph's had a tailor shop, a shoemaker shop, a bakery, a laundry and a farm. We used to darn our own socks and jerseys (sweaters). I don't know if any of the boys learnt a skill or a trade that they could usefully take with them after leaving the school. The only thing industrious about those schools was their throughput, with about 50,000 boys passing through them over time.

The Brothers
There were usually about nine or ten Christian Brothers in St. Joseph's. The numbers would vary depending on availability. On balance I would say that the majority were decent or at least harmless, but the others could be variously described as ruthless, wicked, evil, stupid or just plain cruel. It is sad to say that the latter category not only left the strongest and the most indelible impression on me and the other boys, but I firmly believe that they did lasting psychological damage to some of the boys. I will refer to four of the worst Brothers as A, B, C and D respectively.

I honestly think **Brother A** was mentally unstable. He had false teeth that he played with like a horse playing with a bit. When he started to get angry he would push his dentures out and draw them back in again. He ran the kitchen and the refectory (dining area). There was understandably a lot of noise with up to 150 boys in the refectory. The noise level would be low initially but inexorably rise as the boys competed to be heard. As the noise level increased, A's stress level would rise and he would play with

"The Runner"

his teeth with increasing speed. This was accompanied by a whining noise as if suffering from a chronic headache. These were strong danger signs and as the noise level rose to an unbearable level for him he would explode into a rage, pull out his strap and run from table to table beating boys indiscriminately. The noise level would suddenly drop, and A would withdraw towards the kitchen.

On many occasions, Brother A would single out a boy for special attention. He would dash up to the boy and pull him up out of the bench by his ears. He would throw the boy to the floor and beat his bare legs with the leather strap. I was unfortunate to be one of his victims on several occasions. On one occasion after beating me on the floor he pulled me by my hair back on to my feet and slapped me across the face repeatedly. Next thing I felt something pop in my ear. I was to discover later that he had perforated my ear drum.

Brother B ran the school farm. He was a big man and he looked and acted thuggish, and all the boys were scared of him. On one occasion I, along with two other boys, were sent to do some weeding on the farm. It was a sunny day and by jumping up we could see the bay over the sea wall. One of the boys suggested that if we climbed up on the greenhouse we would get a better view. All three of us climbed to the roof of the greenhouse in eager anticipation of the scenic view. The greenhouse comprised steel and glass and we were careful to avoid putting any pressure on the glass. Suddenly Brother B appeared and as soon as he spotted us he started running towards us. We knew we were in big trouble, and we scampered down as quickly as we could, but we were cornered by B. He grabbed the first boy and punched him mercilessly and then threw him to the ground and kicked him for good measure. He did likewise with the second boy and then came to me. I expected the same treatment, but surprisingly he wrapped one arm around my head as if in a wrestling grip. He then pressed the heel of his free hand against my nose in an

"The Runner"

attempt to crush it. I was filled with horror at the thought that he was trying to crush my nose, but somehow I had the presence of mind to throw my legs up in the air. The dead weight of my body caused my head to slip from his grasp and I fell to the ground. He kicked me repeatedly, but I accepted the kicking as a welcome alternative to being permanently disfigured.

I suffered from nightmares for a long time after that incident and I shuddered with fear whenever B came anywhere near me. I couldn't understand why a so called "Christian" Brother would try to do such a thing. There was a boy in the school with a terribly disfigured nose and I was left to wonder if that was the result of cruelty by someone like Brother B.

Brother B became known as the school "Enforcer" in that other Brothers got him to dole out severe punishments whenever they didn't have the stomach to do it themselves.

Brother C was incredibly cruel. Our football boots were kept in a boot room, and he would take boys into the boot room where they were trapped and he would beat them mercilessly. I saw many boys emerge from that room beaten black and blue. I kept as far away as possible from Brother C and somehow managed to avoid such a terrible beating.

A boy named Sweeney joined my class in the 3rd year. He was ten years old and it was obvious that Sweeney was troubled, more so than the rest of the boys. I suppose that to some extent most of us had been traumatised and we were each learning to cope and to recover as best we could from whatever caused our trauma. Many of us became withdrawn and introverted to allow us time to slowly emerge into the normal world. However, Sweeney was shut down to a greater extent than any of the other boys. He had a stammer, which made it hard to understand him at times. He was treated with sympathy by the lay teacher in class 2, but his life took a turn for the worse from class 3 onwards because those

"The Runner"

classes were taught by Brothers who saw sympathy as weakness, and the Brothers felt they had to be seen as authoritarian. Misspelt words or incorrect answers were often punished with one or two slaps of the leather and it was perfectly normal for boys to cry when such punishment was doled out. However, Sweeney seemed odd in that he never cried no matter how many slaps he got. Brother C was the teacher in that class and he took it as a personal affront that Sweeney didn't cry. He started to bring Sweeney to the front of the class to punish him and to make an example of him. Over a period of weeks the beatings started with two slaps that progressed to four slaps and then to six slaps. Sweeney would grimace but he would never cry. Most of us found this very disturbing and we pleaded with Sweeney to cry, even to just pretend to cry, but he wouldn't or couldn't. We were left to wonder where this would stop, but C just got more and more angry with Sweeney. One day he brought Sweeney to the front of the class and started to apply the strap with as much force as he could muster. I closed my eyes and held my hands over my ears in an attempt to shut out the horrible scene in front of me, and after what seemed like an eternity I heard a whimper. I looked up and tears started to flow from Sweeney's eyes as he started to cry. I started to cry. Several of us started to cry.

That incident haunted me for many years and it still brings tears to my eyes when I recall it. I have no doubt that Sweeney was psychologically damaged by that event, possibly irreparably so.

Brother D was a pervert. He ran the sixth class. He would often sit behind his desk at the front of the class as he checked the results of tests. He would call up a boy to stand beside him. He would smile at the boy as he took a sweet out from under the lid of the desk. He would beckon the boy to come closer and he would then move the sweet towards the boy. He would entice the boy to take the sweet and as the boy came closer D would run his hand up and down the boy's bare leg. Drawing the boy closer and moving the sweet closer to the boy he would then move his hand up into the boy's short trousers in an attempt to touch his privates. On one occasion a boy pulled away abruptly and Brother D's face went into contortions. He then shouted at the boy that his work was terrible and stood up and pulled the boy over to another bench. He bent the boy over the bench and beat his behind with the strap. It is little wonder that some boys chose to take the sweet. I was fortunate that I was not pretty enough to be summoned to Brother D's desk, but I lived with the fear that I might.

I was subjected to many beatings during my early years at St. Joseph's, but my worst beating would not come close to the beatings meted out to some of the boys. As I got older I suppose I got smarter and I learned how to avoid beatings. However, those physical beatings were to be replaced by what I might term psychological beatings in that every time I saw a boy being cruelly punished it would turn my stomach and leave me with a terrible sense of helplessness at such wanton cruelty. As we observe so too do we unwittingly absorb, and we are then left with a residual memory of an event. That absorption has left me haunted by terrible deeds that I observed.

Referring to those people as A, B, C and D instead of naming them helps me to avoid making them even more vivid in my mind.

The Brothers deemed it an act of defiance if a boy made eye contact with them, punishable with a beating, so the boys became conditioned to avoiding eye contact. This became so engrained in me that I found it very difficult to make eye contact with people for many years after leaving the School. I found it extremely difficult to overcome that conditioning, and unfortunately my difficulty was often interpreted as evasiveness or guilt. It's comical to think of it now, but I was often picked for a bag search when coming through arrivals at airports because I would avoid looking at customs officers.

"The Runner"

Food, Glorious Food
The refectory had twelve tables with up to 14 boys at each table. One of the older boys was designated as a Monitor, and he was responsible for maintaining some sort of order at the table. Breakfast usually comprised of a bowl of porridge and two slices of pre-buttered bread. It was called pre-buttered even though the spread was margarine or dripping (fat). The bread was stacked on two plates placed equidistant from each end of the table. The prayer before meals was the Grace. It went:

"Bless us o Lord
For these thy gifts
Which of thy bounty
We are about to receive
Through Christ, Our Lord
Amen."

In many cases Brother A got us to repeat the Grace because it had been said too fast for his liking. In truth our reciting of the Grace would have left the "Galloping Major" stranded in the stalls. It usually started slowly enough, but it rapidly picked up speed and ended as a sprint to the finish. Why? Because the word "Amen" released a wave of arms and hands as boys snatched bread off the plates at lightning speed. In some cases two boys would snatch at the same slice and tear it apart. The bits were discarded as they switched to still intact full slices. The rule was that every boy would get two slices of bread, but invariably the big boys got the crusts and the thick slices and the small boys got whatever was left. I remember trying to join up pieces of bread like piecing parts from a jigsaw puzzle to see if the bits actually made up two slices, but there was nothing to be done if they didn't. I quickly realised that the worst place to sit was at the end of a table because the plate of bread was barely reachable from there, but that was where the smallest boys were always placed. In time I would move up the table and my slices of bread would get thicker and fuller.

"The Runner"

Dinner varied from stew to bacon and cabbage or sausages and mashed potatoes. In addition to cabbage, the other most common vegetable was turnip. It was "de rigueur" to leave a clean dinner plate. However, I often found it difficult to eat the cabbage because of the presence of slugs. They might have been dead, but I had fears that if I ate a piece of cabbage with a slug in it, the slug would come back to life in my stomach and eat my insides.

I couldn't eat turnips or parsnips because of the dreadful taste triggered by an allergic reaction. Those two vegetables were often cooked and mashed together and served on the plate. I would get a terrible reaction as soon as I tasted them, and Brother A would beat me for not eating that awful mix. He took it as a personal affront to his cooking skills, but he was too ignorant to understand that I genuinely had a problem with those vegetables. One day he tried to force feed me with them, and after forcing a couple of spoons of the mash down my throat he was shocked when I vomited all over the place. He smacked me in disgust and made me clean up the mess, but he never tried to force me to eat vegetables again.

We rarely had enough food to fill our bellies and most of the boys including myself were small for our age and as thin as rakes. A doctor used to come to the school once a year to check on the boys. He prescribed cod liver oil and malt for the boys that he considered vitamin deficient. I hated the taste of cod liver oil, but the nurse administering it told me to pinch my nose and just swallow quickly so as to minimise any taste. On the other hand, the malt had a lovely, sweet taste and I could never get enough of that.

Local Heroes
As a special treat the boys were occasionally taken to Pearse Stadium to watch Galway play football against other county teams, and we could see our heroes on the pitch.

"The Runner"

In 1956 Galway beat Cork to win the GAA All Ireland Football Championship. There was no TV in those days so we listened on the radio to the match commentary, and we screamed with delight when Galway won.

A large photo of the team was put on display in the school for posterity. Boys need heroes, and these were our heroes.

The team was:
Joe Young, Jack Kissane, Gerry Kirwin, Mick Greally,
Mattie McDonagh, Tom Dillon, Frank Evers, Sean Purcell,
Billy O'Neill, Jack Mangan, Gerry Daly, Frank Stockwell,
Jack Mahon, Jackie Coyle, Sean Keeley.

One day the Brothers took us to the main hall in the school and we were told that two special people had come to talk to us. They were Sean Purcell and Mattie McDonagh. We were amazed that they would come to our school, and we were totally awestruck as they talked about how Galway had won the All-Ireland Final in 1956. We prayed that they would win it again soon, but that was to take quite some time. They gave advice on how important it was to work hard at sport and at classes, and then they accepted questions from the boys. I was far too shy to ask a question, but I still recall the impression they made on me that day in that they made us believe that if you try hard enough, you can achieve success.

"The Runner"

Darning Socks & Jumpers
In those early days socks and jumpers were made from wool and holes would appear in them in the normal course of wear and tear. An elderly woman ran the laundry and she also had responsibility for repairing the socks and jumpers. We all had to learn how to darn. The wool for repairs came in a big loop which was held in two outstretched arms and the wool was unwound from the loop by another boy and rolled into balls of about six inches in diameter. This prevented the wool from getting tangled up. Darning needles were supplied and the younger boys generally repaired the socks and the older boys usually repaired the jumpers because they had larger hands that could hold the jumpers. I became quite skilled at darning and I was very proud of my needlework. Some of the boys struggled with darning and the woman would beat them repeatedly as if that would improve their darning skills. When it became obvious that some boys would never acquire that skill, they were given the role of forming the wool into balls.

Sunday Walks
The Sunday walk involved a Brother taking the boys for a walk around the Salthill area for an hour or two, typically to Barna and back, or up Threadneedle Road and on to Rahoon and then back to the school. Up to my arrival at St Joseph's I had been locked away from the world, but now I was about to see life on the outside of a school for the first time.

On those first Sunday walks in 1954 I saw men and women dressed in their Sunday best clothes. I had seen men riding bicycles before, but I had never seen a woman riding a bicycle up till then. Most shops were closed, but some shops were open and sold newspapers and sweets and ice creams. I could only dream of having an ice cream. There were few cars on the street and occasionally a big bus would go by with the passengers staring at us, and we staring back at them. Salthill was lively and exciting

"The Runner"

compared to our dull world and the Sunday walks soon became a highlight of my life at St Joseph's.

The boys were formed into a column with the youngest boys placed at the front and the oldest boys at the rear where the Brother was also located. I was at the front initially and off we would go like an eager pack of huskies with no notion of where we were going other than to turn left at the front gate and head for the promenade. As we made our way along the Prom the line would sometimes get stretched but another hundred yards or so would soon slow us down as we ran out of steam. A bigger boy would come running up from the rear to tell us to turn left or right as the Brother ordered and he would then race back to the rear of the group. Later he would come running up again with another instruction - slow down, speed up, turn left or turn right, etc., and then he would dash back to the rear again. I was to learn that this boy was referred to as a "Runner" and he was selected for that job because of his running speed. I admired and envied the "Runner" and wondered if one day I might become a "Runner", but I had to put such foolish notions out of my head as I struggled to climb to the top of Threadneedle Road at age seven.

On one Sunday walk as we headed towards Barna we saw some men crossing the road and they were carrying bags with what looked like sticks hanging out of the bags. They were dressed strangely with baggy trousers that were tucked into their socks, and they wore peaked caps. We thought they looked very odd and we laughed at this sight, but the men were very serious. We watched them go through a gate into the field on our left, so we assumed they were going to do some digging in the field and we didn't envy them in the least. We were out walking and enjoying our two hours of relative freedom. I was too small at that time to see over the wall running alongside the field, so I never got to see those men actually digging it. However, I imagined it would be hard work for them and so I felt a little bit sorry for them to be doing such hard work on a Sunday.

"The Runner"

One of the boys said that the men were golfers and that they were going to play golf in the field. I'd never heard of golf, but I was very curious as to how the men might play this weird sounding game. Why not Gaelic football or hurling or even tennis? On some occasions we would hear the men shout "Four".
I assumed that was some sort of score and maybe they were trying to get a six or a seven for all I knew.

One day we saw a movie in the school with a scene showing people playing golf, and finally I had some sense of how this game was played. We thought the movie was very funny because people kept shouting "Four" and the golfers would duck down and put their hands over their heads for protection against errant golf balls. One of the Brothers explained that they were shouting "FORE". He went on to explain that the game of golf had been invented in Scotland, and that when the ball was hit in the wrong direction and likely to hit someone, the golfer would shout FORE to warn the players ahead. He went on to explain that the reason they shouted "FORE" and not "FOUR" was that it was an abbreviation of the word "AFORE", meaning ahead, and that over time this had been shortened to "FORE. This was my first golf lesson, and I took from it a word that I would put to great use on hundreds of occasions in the distant future.

I then realised that those people that were crossing the road on our Sunday walks to Barna were golfers, and far from being pitied they were to be envied. We were told that these were amongst the richest and most important people in Galway, being doctors, solicitors, businesspeople, and even Bishops and priests, and only such important people were allowed to play golf. Well, I had no notions of ever playing golf because I expected to be digging fields when I grew up.

One of the things that struck me when we returned to the school was the eerie silence around the place which was in huge contrast to the cacophony of noise that normally reverberated off the buildings. The unnatural silence would initially be broken by the arrival of younger boys and would quickly return to its multi decibel levels when the bigger boys arrived. I imagine that the Brothers who remained at the school during those walks found the silence a welcome respite.

The Sunday Walk
The Sunday Walk takes us outside
To a world where others reside
Bustling with people going to and fro
A world that we may never know

People scurry here and there,
Stopping briefly just to stare
And we like animals in a zoo
Can't help but stare at them too
(We): Where will they go, who will they see?
(They): I bet those boys would like to be free

Soon our walk comes to an end
And in the school we just pretend
The outside world is not for real
To us that world holds no appeal.

We had to accept that our world was our reality and that the outside world was irrelevant to us.

As the years went by Val and I progressed back towards the middle of the Sunday walk with new and younger boys replacing us at the front. I was delighted when Val was selected to be the runner at age 15. He would dash towards the front of the column of boys with utter determination and casually trot back towards the rear and give me a knowing smile as he passed me on the return leg. I was so proud of him, but I also envied him. Only the best were chosen for that prestigious role.

"The Runner"

Sport
The school playground was the main arena for casual sports where the boys would play "tag" or football or handball, etc. Organised sports were mainly Gaelic football and hurling team games and these were played on the school pitches. Everybody wanted to be on a team, no matter what the sport was. To be selected gave a feeling of inclusiveness and a certain status. Only boys aged 12 and older could play hurling, possibly due to the limited supply of hurley sticks. A group of boys would be selected to play hurling, but I would have to wait a long time before I would be entrusted with a hurley stick, so I could only aspire to play football initially. The boys for football were usually placed into two groups, those aged up to 11 and those aged 12 and older. Typically the supervising Brother would pick out two of the older boys in each group to act as team captains to select their own teams from their group. Captain A would be given first call, and he would pick out the best available boy. Then Captain B would pick out his best choice, and that would continue until they both had a team of 15.

As an eight-year-old I had no chance of being picked, and I and the other unchosen ones would be left to watch the teams play their match. Although I was disappointed not to be selected, that feeling was assuaged as I watched Val play. I would race up and down the sideline encouraging him and cheering him on. I was so proud of him and I prayed that one day I would be selected to go on a team with him, but that seemed highly unlikely that first year. One day in the following summer I was delighted when a Captain selected me to join his team. I proudly stepped forward to join my team. The fact that I was the last available boy was irrelevant. I was on a team at last. We were sent to the boot room to get our kit and tog out. I had a shirt that was way too big for me, shorts that covered most of my legs, and football boots that were at least two sizes too big for me, but none of that mattered to me as I gamely plodded on to the pitch with my heart bursting with pride. The match started and I soon got a lesson about Gaelic

"The Runner"

football. Whenever the ball came near me I was flattened to the ground by an opponent. In competitive sport winning is all that matters, and I quickly learned that I would be steamrolled if I got in the way of anyone in the opposing team. I didn't get a touch of the ball throughout that first match and I was beginning to regret being selected for the team. Years later I would learn that you shouldn't pray too hard for what you want because you might regret it when you get it.

As time went by I got bigger and better and I learned how to look after myself. I grew to love sport and a competitive streak took root within me in those early days. It still resides within me.

In 1960 I had turned 13 years old and I was picked for the school under 14 football team. We played against local teams like the Claddagh and St Enda's. On my first match I was shocked at how big our opponents were in comparison to us. They had no trouble muscling us out of their way as they went on to thrash us. However, over time we got bigger, better and more confident and we started to win some matches. I would play with the under 14's for one more year and then progress to the under 16 team.

The Sea
Every summer we would be taken to the beach at lower Salthill to go swimming. Although I was a poor swimmer I enjoyed splashing around in the sea water. I was fascinated by the crabs and the cockles and mussels that were to be found on or under the rocks. I became quite good at picking up crabs between my thumb and forefinger and throwing them at other boys.

Occasionally when there was a full tide we would see fish jumping in the water as if gasping for air. On one particular summer's evening it was very humid and there was a full tide so we only had to go out a few yards for the water to be waist high. Suddenly we were surrounded by fish swimming close to the surface. Some

"The Runner"

boys reached down to the seabed to pick up stones to throw at the fish, so I did likewise. Amazingly I hit a fish and I either stunned it or killed it such that it was now floating in the water right in front of me. I tried to grab it but it slipped out of my hands. I managed to lift it out of the water with outstretched hands and brought it to the beach, and after changing into my clothes I wrapped it in a towel. It was a good-sized fish, about 10 inches long. When we got back to the school I took it to the Brother's kitchen. They had a lady cook and I offered her the fish. She said it was a mackerel, and she thanked me for it. I was so proud of my achievement at catching a fish.

The next day we went into the refectory for dinner. I was seated at a table at the end of the refectory and facing the main door. I was astonished when just after Grace was finished, the lady cook walked into the refectory and started scanning all the faces. Brother A was equally shocked and queried: "What's this, what's this?" The lady cook just ignored him and suddenly she spotted me and started to make a bee line towards me. I nearly died with embarrassment as my face lit up like a Belisha beacon.* She placed a covered dish down in front of me and lifted the lid to reveal the beautifully cooked mackerel, and she said, "You caught it so now enjoy it." She looked at Brother A as if to say, "That's his. Keep away."

Brother A was speechless but he knew not to cross her, after all he would depend on her for his own meals. The smell of the fish was amazing, and the taste was heavenly. Suddenly I was the most popular boy at my table as the other boys begged me for a piece of the fish. I duly cut up little pieces and passed them to my newfound appreciative friends. We all got a hint that day of what good food could taste like, but we had no notions that we would have such an experience again.

Belisha was the UK Minister for Transport in 1934 and he added an orange flashing light at pedestrian crossings to reduce accidents. The orange globe became known as a Belisha Beacon.

"The Runner"

Cinema
The school had a cinema in which we watched movies, but occasionally we would be taken out to a local cinema, either the Estoria or the Savoy. We all loved the movies and after most movies we couldn't wait to play out the main characters in the playground. Nobody wanted to play the bad guys, including me. I wanted to be John Wayne (not tall enough), but I got to play Shane (Alan Ladd) from the movie of the same name. At the end of that movie Shane is riding away after killing all the bad guys (including Jack Palance), and the young boy Joey shouts after him, "Shane, Shane, come back. I love you Shane."

As I rode across the playground on my imaginary horse one of the boys shouted, "Shane, Shane, come back." I looked back to wave to him, only to bump into the duty Brother. A quick smack across the head soon brought me back to reality.

Val loved to impersonate John Wayne, but with a twist when he would say in a tough no-nonsense voice:

"Get off your horse and drink your milk!".

And I would reply in an equally tough no-nonsense voice:

"I'll get off my horse but I won't drink that milk".
With that we would face off, count to three and then draw our imaginary guns and shoot. Val always won those duels because he insisted on winning and he was my older brother so he got his way.

Cinema was a wonderful escape from reality, albeit fleetingly.

Schooling
At St. Joseph's our subjects were limited to English, Irish, Maths and History classes, but occasionally we would also learn some poetry. It was commonplace for boys to be beaten in class for

"The Runner"

producing an incorrect answer. This happened most often in the Maths classes, but also quite frequently in the Irish classes. Irish was my weakest subject, so I had to endure the punishment that was doled out for some incorrect answers. The Brothers thought they could beat a love of Irish into the boys but they were actually beating it out of us. Most beatings involved hitting boys on the hands with straps, but some Brothers would pull down a boy's trousers to administer beatings on the behind. This added hugely to the sense of shame. As I grew older I became more aware of the futility of beatings. I can't think of anyone who became smarter because of them, but I do know that the fear and shame they instilled in some boys made them less capable of absorbing what they were being taught. They understandably developed a fear and a hatred for the Brothers.

"You fools, you fools, why could you not see the damage you were doing."

Except for Irish I came to enjoy most classes and I developed a hunger for learning, my best subject being Maths followed closely by English. This hunger for learning would stay with me for life.

When boys finished schooling at St Joseph's, usually at age 14, it was normal practice to spend the following two years working on the farm or in the laundry or the kitchen. Val was sent to work on the farm and he tended to the school's two plough horses, Charlie and Paddy, cleaning out their stables and ensuring that they had feed. When Val turned 16 he was placed with a farming family in Moylough, Galway. He was treated very badly by the family and as soon as he had enough money he made his way to Dublin to stay with Pearl before continuing his journey to England to join Dennis. Ethel had joined Dennis in England two years earlier. I knew that when I turned 16 and placed with a family, I too would make my way to England as soon as I could.

"The Runner"

Visiting Priest
The same priest came to the school to say mass every morning, but once a year he would take a week's holiday and be replaced by a relief priest. One year, the relief priest turned out to be a Father Egan. The regular priest always seemed to be very sombre and generally just going through the motions of mass in an automatic way. In contrast, Fr. Egan seemed to delight in his role and made interesting or funny comments most days to lighten the mood in the chapel.

On his final day he told an interesting story about one of the altar boys. The mass was said in Latin and there is a part in the mass where the altar boy has to recite:

"Mea Culpa, Mea Culpa, Mea Maxima Culpa."

Father Egan said that he wasn't sure that the altar boy was saying those words correctly so on the final morning he made a point of leaning over towards the boy to hear more clearly what he was saying. It transpired that he was saying:

"Me a cowboy, me a cowboy, me a Mexican cowboy."

The Blessed Virgin Mary
Each classroom had a statue of the Blessed Virgin Mary in a glass cabinet secured to the wall about five feet from the floor, and every May the statues would be decorated with blue and white ribbons which were formed into a twirl, like streamers. When I was in the fifth year, I and another boy were assigned the task of decorating the statue in our class. This was a great honour, a huge sign of confidence in our ability to do a good job. We were to do the work on a Saturday so that the decorated Mary would be seen first thing on Monday morning.

"The Runner"

We needed to stand on a table to reach the cabinet and the statue. The statue was about four feet tall and the cabinet had a side door to give access to the statue. I suggested to the other boy that we take the statue out and place it on the floor so that we could give the cabinet and Mary a good clean (one of my early signs of thoroughness). The other boy agreed. We had seen this done before so I assumed it would be straight forward and I volunteered to take the statue out and pass it to him as he stood on the floor. I wasn't much taller than the statue and it turned out to be heavier than I expected. As I took the statue out of the cabinet I discovered that it was very dusty and the Blessed Virgin Mary slipped out of my grasp and on to the floor and broke into smithereens. Years later I would be reminded of that moment by a scene from "Only Fools and Horses" where a chandelier was accidentally dropped to the floor.

I gasped in horror at what I had just done and the other boy became hysterical and started jumping up and down and screaming at me about the terrible beating we would both get. I clambered down from the table and gazed at the pieces of Mary scattered all over the floor. I too gave some thought to the impending beating, but suddenly a flash of Divine inspiration struck me as I came up with a cunning plan (like Baldrick years later in Black Adder). There was a similar statue in a cabinet in a storeroom on the other side of the playground. I would replace our disintegrated Mary with that one. The other boy said I was mad, but I said boldly:

"Come on, we can do this."

I had visions of us wrapping Mary II in a sheet and the pair of us carrying her across the playground, and how we would both pray to Mary II that none of the other boys would barge into us and cause her to be smashed too. We went over to the storeroom and there was Mary II looking down on us expectantly. As luck would have it there was a wheelbarrow in the storeroom and we had no

"The Runner"

problem finding a big white sheet. I had learned my lesson with Mary I as I again volunteered to remove the statue from the cabinet. This time I handed her ever so carefully to my newfound accomplice in crime and he stood Mary II on the floor. So far so good. My accomplice was as nervous as a kitten but I said, "Don't worry. This will work out just fine. Be positive."

We put some padding in the wheelbarrow and placed Mary II gently into her chariot and then placed the sheet over her. I volunteered to wheel the barrow across the playground and I told my friend to keep the other boys in the playground well away from the barrow. There was a duty Brother walking around the playground and I prayed to Mary II to keep him looking away from us as we made our way across the playground. We made it back to our classroom without detection, and now it was a simple matter of cleaning the cabinet, putting up the decorations and placing Mary II in her new home. When we were finished we both stood back to admire our handiwork and I couldn't help but notice Mary smiling approvingly at me. The other boy said:

"Wardy, you're a genius."

In that moment, I thought I was.

On the Monday morning we all went into the classroom and the boys and the Brother looked up and admired Mary II. The Brother praised me and my friend for the great work we had done and then said, "Let's all say the Rosary to Mary."

A couple of days went by without anyone noticing anything but later that week I was summoned to a room by the Brother in charge of our class. My accomplice was nowhere to be seen, but I knew I was in trouble.

"Did you break the statue of the Blessed Virgin Mary in our class and replace it with the statue from the storeroom?"

"The Runner"

He asked that question in the full knowledge that he knew the answer, so I decided to come clean and I told him that it was a terrible accident and that I was truly sorry. I fully expected that he would hand me over to Brother B, the "Enforcer", but he told me to put my hand out and he gave me three slaps of the leather on each hand and sent me on my way. I considered myself very lucky to get off so lightly, and as I reflect on it now I sense that he may have had a suppressed admiration for my creativity in my attempt to mitigate a very difficult problem, or he just didn't want me to be brutalised by Brother B.

The Nurse
That same summer I was playing a hurling match in St Joseph's and I was struck in the left knee with a hurley. I was crippled and quickly taken to the infirmary to be attended to by the resident nurse. My knee was badly swollen and extremely painful. Despite the pain, the nurse manipulated my knee and told me that it was not broken and just badly bruised. She kept me in the infirmary overnight but the following day the swelling seemed to get worse and she said she had called for a local doctor to see me. A doctor arrived that evening and examined my knee and he told the nurse to apply a cold compress to it to bring the swelling down, and then he left. The nurse told me that she had expected the doctor to lance my knee and squeeze out the pus to minimise the risk of infection. An hour or so after the doctor left she came to my bed with a basin of very hot water. She heated a dressing pad and placed it on my knee and I yelped at the pain. She did this a couple of times and then told me to grab the bars at the head of the bed. She told me to be brave and to stare at a light in the ceiling. Next thing I felt a searing pain that lasted a few seconds, but I managed not to scream. She had lanced my knee and started to squeeze out the pus. She cleaned my knee and wrapped a bandage around it and left me to ponder what had just happened. A few minutes later she came back to me with some toast and jam and a mug of tea and she praised me for being very brave.

"The Runner"

When I had finished the tea and toast she took the tray away and came back a minute later with a sweeping brush. She told me to get out of the bed and sweep the floor. I was shocked. The next morning she got me out of bed again and made me walk around the ward for ten minutes.

At the time I thought that this had been an act of cruelty on her part, but she was simply getting me to use my knee and prevent it getting stiff. Over time I realised that she had done what she thought was best for me and which eliminated the risk of an infection. Within a matter of weeks I was back playing hurling.

Ethnea Tiernan
When I was 13 a scheme was introduced where people outside the school were invited to write to a boy in the school at Christmas and send greetings. The following Christman Val and I received a card from two sisters named Tiernan. The lady who wrote to me was Ethnea Tiernan but I don't recall her sister's name. The Brothers then arranged for us to reply with a "Thank You" card. Val turned 16 the following January and I turned 14 the following March. We both received birthday cards, which was very nice, and we both sent Thank You cards. Val left the school a short time later and I continued to have exchanges with Ethnea Tiernan. I assumed at that time that she was a middle-aged lady, but our correspondence was vetted by the Brothers and we were not allowed to ask personal questions or strike up a close relationship with those people.

I failed to stay in touch with Ethnea when I left the school, and I regret that very much. On starting out to write this book I remembered Ethnea and I wondered if I could track her down, only to discover that she died in 2012 aged 77. She was 25 years old when she started writing to me.

"The Runner"

Brother Egan

Things started to change in the school from around 1961 when a new Brother Superior arrived, Brother Egan. Amazingly, he was the family brother of Father Egan who had previously stood in as a relief priest, so their family had a Christian Brother and a priest who had committed their lives to the Church.

Brother Egan was unlike any Brother I had ever come across. He actually mowed the front lawn all by himself, something we had never seen any other Brother do. He was a keen gardener and he put flowerbeds at the front of the school so that they were visible to the public walking past the main gates. He sometimes got me to help him with planting the flowers and he would tell me the names of the flowers. He treated me as a person and not as a delinquent, and I sensed in him an innate decency that I had never sensed with any other Brother.

Brother Egan turned out to be a moderniser and he did everything he could to transform St Joseph's into something other than an Irish version of a borstal. He shut down the bakery and bought in bread. He shut down the laundry and sent our clothes out to be laundered. He discouraged physical punishment and replaced it with sanctions such as withholding privileges, etc., and he introduced us to underpants and long trousers, both of which felt very strange. In effect, he set about humanising St. Joseph's.

When I turned 14 and finished schooling I fully expected to be put to work on the farm, or worse still in the kitchen with Brother A, but Brother Egan had other ideas. He shocked me when he told me that when the new term started in September, I and five other boys would go out each day to continue our education at the Technical School in the Claddagh. This was to be a whole new experience. I was still chronically shy when I arrived at the Tech for the first time. The place was a complete ruckus of noise and activity and I felt lost. More startling for me was that this was a school for boys and girls, but not with mixed classes. I just didn't

"The Runner"

know how to respond when a girl said hello or asked me a question. I wanted to crawl into my shell and stay there and most of the time I avoided fellow students as much as possible.

In addition to Maths, English and Irish, I would learn basic science, basic electricity, carpentry and metalwork. I couldn't get enough of these new subjects and I threw myself into every lesson or class and they would prove invaluable to me over time.

I had a huge shock the first time I walked into the Maths classroom. The teacher was none other than Jack Mahon, one of the heroes of Galway's All Ireland Football Championship team from 1956. He was not only a great footballer, but he was also a great teacher and he improved my Maths skills enormously. I had now seen up close Sean Purcell, Mattie McDonagh and Jack Mahon from that team, and little was I to know that many years later I would also meet Sean Keeley.

Val made a point of writing to me quite often, and one day he told me that Pearl was getting married and that he was coming back to Ireland for the wedding. A few days before the wedding Brother Egan sent for me and told me that Val had written to him to explain that Pearl was getting married and requesting that I be allowed to go to the wedding in Dublin. Val offered to come over from England and come down to Galway to collect me, take me to the wedding and bring me back to the school the following day. I was astounded. Egan said that he had decided to let me attend the wedding on the basis that Val had given his word that he would bring me back to the school and not take me to England with him. Nothing like this had ever happened in the school before. I was given a new suit, a white shirt and a tie, all on loan.

Sure enough Val collected me on the day before the wedding. We stayed in a B & B in Dublin near to where Pearl lived. She was getting married to a man named Leo. We went to the church and Pearl duly arrived in her beautiful white dress. She looked stunning.

"The Runner"

After the wedding service we went to a hotel for the celebrations. Two middle aged women sitting opposite Val and me at the dinner table enquired as to who we were. Val said that we were Pearl's brothers. One looked at me intently and then turned to her friend and said, "Well, you can see that he came from the other side of the blanket," and the pair of them started laughing. I asked Val what that meant and he told me to ignore the comment. Despite the fact that I was fair skinned and Dennis, Pearl, Ethel, Val and my mother were all tanned looking, that was the first time I sensed that I might somehow be different to them. (I am intrigued that children don't seem to notice differences whereas adults often seem to highlight them in a cruel way.)

As the two women started to drink the free wine they gradually got tipsy. The "blanket" lady had dentures, and at one point she coughed and her dentures came flying out of her mouth and landed on the table. She panicked and fumbled and did everything she could to pick up the dentures and shove them back into her mouth, and suddenly Val and I were the ones laughing at her.

Val took me back to the school the next day and he made a point of thanking Brother Egan for allowing me to attend the wedding. The wedding had a huge impact on me in that I had rarely seen Pearl or Val in such a happy state, and it gave me a sense of the joy that could be experienced in the world beyond the school.

In my final year at St Joseph's, Brother Egan set about trying to introduce boys in their final year to the outside world. One Sunday he selected me and three other boys for his first attempt at this process. He gave each of us a shilling and told us to go around Salthill or Galway for a few hours and get familiar with the outside world and return in three hours. I was somewhat bemused by this as each of us stepped out on to the street and went our separate ways. I don't know why but I sensed that in addition to conditioning us Brother Egan might have been testing us on how we spent the money, so I decided to buy the cheapest

"The Runner"

newspaper I could find and spend the rest of the money on sweets. I had no interest in the newspaper but I hoped it would provide cover for buying the sweets. On arriving back at the school Brother Egan got us together and asked us to tell him what we had spent the money on. The other boys had spent it all on sweets and an ice cream. When he turned to me I showed him the newspaper and said that I had spent the change on sweets. He smiled at me and then scolded the other boys. A month later he repeated the exercise with the same four boys, and that Sunday we all returned to the School with a newspaper!!

Strangely enough, I came to enjoy reading the Sunday paper, especially the sports section.

Within the first year of Brother Egan arriving, Brothers A, B, C and D were all replaced, and the meek and humble Brother Egan reigned supreme.

1962
One day we were all gathered to go to the Estoria cinema to see a new movie. Everyone was saying it would be a great movie and we were all excited at the prospect. Somehow I managed to say or do something that upset the Brother in charge and he told me to report to the kitchen as punishment. I was terribly disappointed not to go to the cinema.

When the boys got back from the Estoria they were all trying to play the lead character. His name was Bond, James Bond, and the movie was called "Doctor No". This was Sean Connery's first movie in that role. The year was 1962, and many years would pass before I would get to see that movie.

1962 was also the year that TV came to St Joseph's. In the winter months we were taken to the school cinema to watch TV. Most of the programs were American, mainly sit coms and westerns.

"The Runner"

My life at St Joseph's was progressing quite well now. I was doing well academically and also at sport. I progressed to the under 16's football team, and the highlight of my footballing career was when we reached the final of the local championship and discovered that the final would be played in Pearse Stadium. This was hallowed ground for me, the place where I had seen my heroes play. Sadly we were beaten in the final, but I will always be able to say that I once played football in Pearse stadium.

One Sunday that summer we gathered for our regular Sunday school walk. I was now near the back of the column of boys. The Brother tapped me on the head and said:

"Ward, you are the Runner today."

I was so eager for my first instruction and when I got it I went racing off to the front of the column like a rabbit on a promise. I ran so fast that I overshot the lead boys and I had to dig my heels in to stop my run.

"Next right, next right", I barked at the three boys at the front of the column. I raced back like a loyal sheepdog seeking approval from its master. To my huge relief the column turned to the right. I was so proud to have followed in the footsteps of Val by progressing to become a "Runner". I imagined the two of us as "Runners" racing to the front of the column side by side, stride for stride and smiling at each other with pride. Who would have thought that the two waifs would one day morph into "Runners".

(On one of our Sunday golf outings I told John Rabbit the story about the "Runner". Little did I expect that a few weeks later John would use it to come up with a sketch depicting "The Runner", and a proposed title for this book. A copy of the original sketch is shown. That sketch was developed into the image on the covers of this book. I am indebted to John for unblocking my resistance to writing the book. Many thanks John.)

"The Runner"

THE RUNNER

Departure

In June 1963 US President John F Kennedy visited Galway. Most of the boys were lined up on the street outside St Joseph's School as his motorcade passed in front of us. He was our hero and here he was, larger than life standing up in his car and waving to us. We were then taken to Eyre Square to hear his speech. It was possibly the first time in my life that I felt proud to be Irish, largely because of his incredible achievement in becoming President of the USA. He was an inspiration to me and made me feel that even boys who spent most of their childhood in Industrial schools could also be achievers.

"The Runner"

A few weeks later I would depart from St Joseph's. I had spent 13 of my first 16 years of life in institutions and I was very anxious about how I would cope in the huge wide world that I was about to enter. However, the prospect of being reunited with Val, and seeing Dennis, Pearl and Ethel again assuaged my sense of foreboding about embarking on the next phase of my life.

I expected to be placed with a farming family, just as Dennis and Val had been, but I was very surprised to be placed with a family in Portumna in south County Galway. They ran a bicycle repair shop, and in fairness I have to say that the family treated me well. However, I now found myself in a totally alien environment. I had freedom, but I didn't know what to do with it. I was socially awkward and ill equipped for this new world. People would try to engage with me but I had no experience in such normal everyday interactions. I felt terribly vulnerable and because of that I erected social barriers to keep people at bay. It would take a long time for me to dismantle those barriers.

Most of the bicycles that were brought in for repair had punctures or chains that had slipped off the gear wheel or malfunctioning brakes, and the owner of the business taught me how to carry out basic repairs. I would find myself alone in the repair shop fixing bicycles most days, but I was content to be left alone. However, customers would come into the shop from time to time and immediately enquire as to who I was and where I had come from. Irish people are tremendously inquisitive, and none more so than those in small rural towns. I just wanted to focus on the bicycles because I didn't know how to deal with people, but they wanted to know all about me. I tried desperately to conceal my past but my interrogators would never let up until they had extracted the facts to their satisfaction.

"The Runner"

"Who are you?"	"I work here"
"What's your name?	"Patsy"
"Patsy what?"	"Patsy Ward"
"Are you a Traveller?*	"No"
"Where are you from?"	"Galway"
"Where in Galway?"	"Galway city"
"What street?"	"Salthill"
"Which school did you go to?	(stalled) – "St Joseph's"
"The Industrial School"	"Yes"

Gotcha

*(*Ward was a name commonly associated with the Traveller community in the West of Ireland, and that community was stigmatised in Ireland at that time.)*

I would blush terribly when the revelation about St. Joseph's had finally been dragged out of me as the customer walked away to leave me to drown in a pool of shame. I had to endure this type of ritual on several occasions and I desperately wanted to get out of Ireland and join Val in England. My primary objective was to get to Pearl's house in Dublin as soon as possible. Within four week I had enough money to pay the bus fare to Dublin. I had written to Pearl and she and Leo had arranged to meet me at the bus stop in Dublin. I said goodbye to the family in Portumna, and as I sat on the bus I had mixed feelings about leaving them. They had tried to support me on leaving the School, but I just knew that I had to get to England to join Val and Dennis.

Pearl and Leo looked after me very well despite living in a small flat with a baby boy. Val came over from England in August 1963 and I was delighted to see him. I mentioned to him that Pearl was sick most days and Val said that she was pregnant. I didn't know what the word meant and I asked him to explain it. He said that Pearl was expecting a baby and that it was normal to get sick sometimes until the baby arrived. This was all new to me and I

"The Runner"

just thought that Val was so worldly wise and I knew nothing. A couple of days after Val arrived we boarded the overnight boat for Liverpool. Nothing could have prepared me for that sea crossing. We sat in a large area below the main deck with seating fitted all along the steel walls (bulkheads) which were dripping with condensation. The weather was stormy and the sea was choppy, and once the boat headed into the open sea it was buffeted and tossed around like a tin can. Passengers started to get seasick and they rushed to the toilets.

Gradually more passengers became sick and the crew raced around the place handing out paper bags for people to be sick into, but soon there weren't enough bags to go around. The toilets were full of passengers being sick and others queueing outside to get in. The stench in the room was awful and it soon made me sick, and I like so many others could only vomit on to the floor. Passengers were now slipping and falling and cursing at their misfortune. Val was violently sick, so much so that the crew took him out and put him in a bunk bed. We discovered later that we had travelled to Liverpool on a cattle boat.

When we arrived in Liverpool we had to find a toilet to clean up and we then made our way by train to Rugeley in Staffordshire where Dennis lived. It was Saturday 17 August 1963.

Reflections:

A Failed System
I am unclear as to why those State institutions were set up other than the fact that they were an expedient way to address a social problem of the children of abandoned or single mothers. If one of the objectives was to produce patriotic Catholic men and women who would serve Ireland's needs, then I can only see that as an abject failure. In the case of my family, four of the five who were incarcerated emigrated to England. It has been speculated that up

"The Runner"

to 80% of all of the boys from State institutions emigrated, and our family record gave credence to that claim.

Fear and Power
Over time I have come to realise that one person's fear is another person's power. The Christian Brothers ruled by fear, and our fear empowered them. The Catholic Church also ruled by fear, threatening us with eternal damnation if we didn't conform to their teachings. When we overcome the fear, we take away their power.

Stigma and Shame
There was undoubtedly a terrible stigma associated with boys who came from State institutions like St Joseph's. A powerful feeling of shame was instilled in us over many years by the Brothers who made us feel that we had been sent to the School because we were guilty of bad behaviour. We were sinners who were indelibly stained and there was to be no redemption for us other than ever-lasting prayer and penance. On leaving St Joseph's it quickly became obvious that this stigma existed well beyond the walls of those institutions, but it was now reinforced by my own sense of guilt and the accompanying shame. As I started to make my way in the world beyond the School I despaired that I was doomed to a miserable life weighed down by my negative emotions and the oppressive forces of an ignorant society.

Light in the Darkness – Hope amidst Despair
At the time of writing I am amazed to realise that 70 years have passed since I left Letterfrack. Those early years there were filled with fear and trepidation and a sense of despair, but Val kept me going in Letterfrack. He was my light in that never ending darkness.

In St Joseph's, decent people emerged to serve as a counterweight to the insensibility of some of the Brothers. People like **Brother Egan, the lady cook, and the nurse.** Their acts of kindness are forever etched in my mind.

"The Runner"

Seeing and hearing people like **Sean Purcell, Mattie McDonagh** and **President John F Kennedy** inspired me and gifted me with the possibility that despite my start in life, I too might succeed if I strove to do so.

Ethnea Tiernan, who wrote to a young boy in a simple act of kindness.

The memory of those people has stayed with me to this day and I believe they imbued me with a sense of how we should treat our fellow humans.

In the year 2000 an investigation was made into the treatment of boys at St. Joseph's. The resultant report can be seen at:

St Joseph's / Salthill Industrial School, Galway, Co. Galway, Republic of Ireland (childrenshomes.org.uk/GalwayStJoseph)
WARNING: It makes for shocking and depressing reading.

"The Runner"

Chapter 2 – A New Life In England

Val and I made our way by train to Rugeley and finally arrived at Dennis' house at around midday on Saturday 17 August 1963. Dennis greeted me wildly and gave me a powerful bear hug that almost squeezed the life out of me. Later that day Val made his way to Stafford where he lived and worked.

Dennis and his wife Pat had a two-year-old daughter and they lived in a small two up two down house. Everything seemed strange to me as I tried to make sense of this new world. The house was located near a railway bridge and every few hours a train would trundle over the bridge and the windows in the house would rattle. That afternoon Dennis took me for a walk around the town to familiarise me with my new surroundings. One of the first things I noticed was the local English accent. It was not what I had been conditioned to expect from watching British movies. Rugeley was about 25 miles from Birmingham, and Dennis explained that people from Birmingham were known as "Brummies" and they had a "Brummy" accent. Another big town in that area was Wolverhampton, which also had a distinctive accent. It seems that the Rugeley accent was a mixture of those two accents.

Rugeley had a population of about 19,000 people then and the main industry was coal mining. The town was dominated by huge chimney stacks at the local power station that was fed with coal from the mines. The chimneys spewed out smoke and steam that left a near permanent blanket of contaminated moisture hanging over the town whenever the wind didn't blow. The summer sun could break though that blanket, but on foggy or misty days it would be near impenetrable and make breathing difficult. This was my first exposure to air pollution, and I found myself thinking of a poem by William A Byrne:

"The Runner"

"The Bog Land"
"Purple is the heather
God gave the bogland brown
But man has made a pall of smoke
That hides the distant town."

I never liked the original first line so I changed it as above. Here is the original version.

> *The purple heather is the cloak*
> *God gave the bogland brown,*
> *But man has made a pall o' smoke*
> *To hide the distant town.*

Rugeley would often be hidden from view by an acrid pall of smoke.

I went to bed early that first night with mixed feelings about having come to England. I felt alienated there and if it wasn't for Val collecting me in Dublin I might never have gone there, and at that time I wondered if that would have been a better choice.

The next morning Dennis took me to the Catholic church for Sunday Mass. He introduced me to other Irish residents of the town and to the parish priest who also happened to be Irish. I was still shy and very unsure of myself and I just wanted to keep to myself, but Dennis was the total opposite and gregarious and clearly well settled in Rugeley.

Pat made a light lunch for us that afternoon and I noticed that Dennis nodded to Pat when we had finished lunch. That was a signal for her to leave us alone, so she went into the kitchen. Dennis said that he needed to explain a few things to me and asked me to sit down.

"The Runner"

He started by saying that he loved me and that nothing would change and he would always treat me as his brother, and then he poured out the family story. Dennis told me that Anthony and I had a different father to all of the older siblings. Needless to say my father was fair skinned which accounted for my fair complexion. Dennis had made his way from Ireland to Rugeley because that was where his father lived at that time, and that was when he discovered that his father was living with another woman who had borne five children with him there. These were all half siblings of Dennis, but of no relationship to me. That family subsequently moved to Manchester and Dennis decided to stay in Rugeley.

Dennis then hit me with a bombshell and told me that our mother was in a mental hospital in Ballinasloe and that she had been there for many years. He never explained how or why she ended up there, and I was left wondering if she had gone mad and if it might be hereditary. Dennis was in such a hurry to blurt everything out that there was no time for me to make sense of anything or to ask questions. He then went on to say that Ethel lived in a village called Handsacre, about five miles away and that Val lived in Stafford which was about eight miles away.

My head was swimming as I tried to absorb and make sense of all of this. I cried my eyes out as Dennis concluded his story. In my rush to judgement I felt that he had betrayed my mother by deciding to reconnect with his father who had abandoned her. Because there was no divorce in Ireland at that time it was not uncommon for men to abandon families by taking the boat to England.

Pat came back into the front room and turned on the TV to act as a distraction. I went up to my room to reflect on everything. I was grief stricken at what had happened to my mother. How were any of us to know that our incarcerations would be followed by hers? A week or so later I met up with Val and he told me that my mother had suffered a nervous breakdown and that she had been

"The Runner"

admitted to St. Brigid's hospital because that was the most expedient thing for the State to do with her at that time. Although many of the boys in St. Joseph's came from Galway, parents and relatives rarely visited them. It was as if there was a deliberate policy of discouraging them from visiting the schools or convents so as to prevent the children from reconnecting with them and becoming troublesome or even running away, which happened several times in St. Joseph's. I could then sense the level of despair that my mother must have felt at having her children so close and yet inaccessible, and how that could have led to her breakdown.

In time the facts that emerged were that my mother had initially been abandoned by Dennis's father. She then met another man who took her and the four children in and offered her financial support. He had two children with her, (me and Anthony) and he then abandoned her. That was in 1950, the year that five siblings were placed in institutions.

My mother would remain in St. Brigid's from 1955 until her death in 1972.

St. Brigid's was built in 1821 as an asylum but from the 1840's it doubled up as a workhouse. How sad it is to reflect on the fact that my mother was born in a workhouse and spent most of her childhood there, and spent the last 17 years of her life in a mental hospital/former workhouse.

At a biological level, Val and I were half-brothers, and the first inkling of that had surfaced at Pearl's wedding, so confirmation of that from Dennis did not come as a complete shock. However, the emotional bond that Val and I had developed for each other in childhood transcended the biological one and would remain the dominant indestructible bond that would prevail throughout our lives.

"The Runner"

My First Job In England
Dennis worked in a company in Lichfield where they shaped and formed steel rods for use in reinforced concrete. The company was located about 8 miles from Rugeley and Dennis told me that he would try to get me a job there. On Monday 19 August we caught a bus to Lichfield and arrived at the site. This was a greenfield site in every sense in that the company was in the process of building a factory there but they had started production in an adjacent field, and their "office" was a Portakabin. Dennis told me to go into the Portakabin and ask for a job. I was petrified of going into the office on my own and I pleaded with Dennis to go in with me, but he refused and simply opened the door and pushed me inside. On entering the cabin I saw several men standing around chatting. They stopped chatting and looked at me and one of them asked me what I wanted. I said I wanted a job. He asked me how old I was and I replied that I was 16 years old. I then said that my brother Dennis worked there and he had told me to come in and ask for a job. It turned out that this guy was a Foreman who could hire and fire people. He said: "Who's Dennis?". I replied that he was my brother and he worked there. The foreman suddenly realised who I was referring to and he said: "Oh, you mean Paddy". I was shocked at the notion that they would call him Paddy, but I just had to accept that. Amazingly he decided to give me a job with the title of "Gofor". I said I didn't know what a "Gofor" was and he said:

"It's simple Paddy. When anyone here wants something they call you and tell you to go for this or go for that and you just fetch it for them."

I was just relieved to get the job and I was then introduced to a production supervisor who would organise my work schedule. I was intrigued that they were now referring to two brothers as "Paddy", but that was their problem.

"The Runner"

My main job was to fetch tools for people, and to collect paperwork and hand it in to the office. My gross pay was £6.00 a week. Which was taxable. I had to give Pat £1.00 a week to pay for lodgings etc, and that didn't leave much for myself after paying bus fares and buying clothes, etc.

The weeks and months went by and winter started to close in but we were still working in the field. Some days were bitterly cold but work continued. The workers would take shelter whenever it rained or snowed and then go back outside when the weather cleared up sufficiently.

I met up with Ethel quite often, and Val made a big effort to come over from Stafford whenever he could. To the extent that it was possible, we were a family again, but I was floating in a sea of confusion.

I was totally ill equipped for this new world. Because of my sheltered life in St Joseph's I was incredibly naive about basic things like social interactions, slang, swearing, how to relate to girls, and I knew nothing about sex. Some people were insulting to me because I was Irish and because in their eyes I was stupid. Some people were nice to me, which left me suspicious. I just didn't know how to react to people. In my sheltered world the good guys wore white and the bad guys wore black, but that did not apply in the real world and this left me in in a constant state of confusion.

Dennis and I used to catch the morning bus to Lichfield and then the evening bus back to Rugeley. However, one day Dennis decided not to go to work and I went to Lichfield on my own. I missed the regular bus home and had to wait an hour or so for the next bus, so I decided to visit Lichfield Cathedral to kill time. I had heard that it was well worth a visit. It was about 5.00pm when I arrived at the cathedral and I started strolling around it admiring the stained-glass windows and the paintings and architecture, etc.

"The Runner"

I noticed a group of five boys aged about 16 or 17 years old also walking around the cathedral. They seemed to be staring at me and then one of the boys said something to another boy and pointed to me. I decided to ignore them, but suddenly a boy came up to me and said:

"Would you care to step outside?"

I told him that I wanted to continue viewing the stained-glass windows and the paintings and that I didn't want to go outside until I had finished my tour of the cathedral. He seemed a bit surprised and then went back to his friends and said something to them. I assumed he was commenting on my Irish accent. They then started laughing and left the cathedral and I spent another 15 minutes continuing my tour. I left the cathedral and there was no sign of the boys as I made my way to the bus station. When I got home I told Dennis about that incident and he said:

"Oh my God. Did you not realise that he wanted to have a fight with you outside the cathedral to impress his mates, and if he wasn't able for you his mates would have jumped on you and beaten you up? He must have thought you were a bit simple when you told him you wanted to continue looking around the cathedral. You don't realise how lucky you are."

That came as a shock to me, and for once in my life I was glad that I had been taken for a simpleton.

In the spring of 1964 I had enough money to go back to Ireland to visit Pearl. When the foreman heard that I was going to Ireland he asked me to buy 200 duty free cigarettes for him. I didn't know anything about duty free cigarettes so I just assumed that cigarettes in Ireland were cheaper than in England. During my trip to Dublin I went into a shop and bought 200 cigarettes and when I returned to work a week later the foreman came to me excitedly and asked me for the cigarettes. I in turn was waiting excitedly for my money back. He had the shock of his life when I told him what I had paid for them and he wanted to know where I had bought them. I told him that I had bought them in a shop in Dublin. The cigarettes turned out to be more expansive in Dublin than they would have been in England, but he just had to pay me what I had paid for them. He called me every name under the sun and said that I was supposed to buy them on the ferry. It was years later that I saw the funny side of that story.

Unsettled
In the spring of 1964 all employees were moved into the new factory building. I turned 17 that March and I was promoted from "Gofor" to working on a machine that formed steel rods into various shapes. Maybe I wasn't a very good "Gofor". The machine work was hard and the working environment was very dusty and noisy, and health and safety were of minor consideration to management. Accidents happened frequently with workers often losing fingers on the fast-moving machines or having hands crushed when steel rods fell down on them. Although my reflexes were good, I came very close to losing a finger on several occasions, and it just seemed a matter of time before my luck would run out. I foolishly started smoking at about that time.

My main problem in 1964 was that Pat had another baby and Dennis told me I would have to find lodgings elsewhere. I spent the next year moving from one place of lodgings to another because people would rarely allow me to stay for more than a few months. I stayed with one couple whose grown up children had moved on, and they treated me very well and wanted me to stay. Unfortunately they lived in a Council house and they received a letter from the Council telling them that they were not allowed to take in lodgers, so I had to move again.

When I turned 18 my salary increased to the standard rate, and now it was worth my while doing overtime. Given that I had little

"The Runner"

more than time to spend anyway, I started working on Saturdays at time and a half, and the occasional Sundays at double time. I felt that if I could keep that up I might possibly be able to rent a flat in Lichfield, but that was still a financial stretch and overtime working depended on demand which was seasonal and not a reliable source of income.

Pat's brother Alan liked to go to the bookies on a Saturday to back the horses. One Saturday he invited me to join him and I sensed that he knew a lot about the horses. He tended to put an each-way bet on every horse he backed, and if they came in the top three he would pick up some winnings. That certainly seemed like a winning strategy to me. He asked me if I would like to back some horses, but I was reluctant to do so given that I knew nothing about horse racing. However, that Saturday happened to be the day of the Oxford-Cambridge boat race, and I told the bookie that I would like to put an each-way bet on Cambridge. He burst out laughing and said: "Are you for real?". Alan then explained that there were only two boats in the race and that it was pointless putting an each way bet on one of them. I didn't know that there were only two boats in that race. I then realised that I also knew nothing about boat racing.

I was very lonely during that period and found it difficult to make friends. I still had an inability to make eye contact with people I didn't know well and this must have made me appear somewhat shifty or evasive, but in any event that further contributed to my sense of alienation. I was still very self-conscious and suffered from very low self-esteem. I wanted to better myself and I considered trying to go to night school, but that would have required me to travel to Stafford or Wolverhampton and the logistics involved in travelling from Lichfield to Rugeley after work and then from Rugeley to Stafford or Wolverhampton made that impossible.

"The Runner"

An elderly couple living in a house just outside Rugeley rented a room to me. They were happy to get the rent and they largely left me alone. One morning I woke up with terrible stomach pains and cramp and they called for a doctor to come and see me. I was in bed when the doctor arrived and they let him into the room. As he asked me to explain my problem it was obvious that he was Irish and he started to enquire about my background. (It turned out that I had severe gastroenteritis). The subsequent conversation started to shape up like another one of those inquisitions in Portumna and I squirmed with embarrassment as I initially tried to conceal details of my background but he persisted in drilling down to get to that ultimate nugget of information. I blushed profusely as I mentioned St Joseph's and he smiled knowingly and then he said something that would have a powerful impact on me.

He asked: Are you embarrassed about your background?"

I replied: "Yes"

He replied "Well, don't be. You have nothing to be ashamed of. You need to realise that you were a victim of circumstance and that you are not to blame for what happened to you and your family. You need to leave that behind you and move on. You have a new life here and most people here won't know and won't care about your background, but you think they do. Stop thinking like that."

For days afterwards I reflected on that conversation, and one day I made a mental flip that enabled me to finally see myself as a victim, a victim of circumstance. The moment I made that flip was the moment that I finally shook off the shackles of guilt and shame that had bound me to my past, and with that came a mental liberation that would change my outlook on life from that moment on. Instead of going through life looking down at the pavement in order to avert my gaze from people, I would start to look straight ahead and take my chances on life, come what may.

"The Runner"

I met a nice girl named Christine and we started dating. We were both 18 years old and we got on really well. She lived with her parents and I still lived in digs. We used to go to local pubs in Rugeley for a drink but we never really had any moments of privacy. One evening she contacted me via a friend and asked me to come around to her house. When I arrived she told me that her parents had gone to the cinema and that we had the house to ourselves. It didn't take long for some heavy petting to start and within minutes we were on the sofa trying to undress while still petting. The whole thing was very clumsy but temperatures were rising and we didn't care. Next thing we heard a key in the latch of the front door and we leapt off the sofa and frantically started to rearrange our clothing as her parents walked in. They looked at us for what seemed like ages but in fact was just a few seconds, and then her dad escorted her mother into the kitchen. He emerged shortly after and I thought I was in for a good beating but he looked at us both and said:

"We need to know if you are getting dressed or undressed because we don't know how long we should stay in the kitchen".

A huge sense of relief swept over me and I spluttered out that I should go, and I made my way hurriedly to the front door.

I met Christine a couple of days later and she said that her parents liked me and if it wasn't for that they would have run me out the door. Christine and I continued to see each other, but we never had exclusive use of her house again.

I was still being shunted from digs to digs and my situation was becoming quite desperate. I couldn't see a way out of this dilemma, but hope encourages us to keep our eyes open to opportunity, and opportunity came about in late 1965.

The UK had been gearing up for a general election for several months and I recall hearing a speech by Harold Wilson, the then

"The Runner"

Labour Party leader, where he said something along the lines that Britain needed to let go of brawn powered industries and replace them with brain powered industries such as electronics. That message resonated with me, but I could only dream of becoming an electronics engineer. A few weeks later I saw a recruitment poster for the Royal Navy (RN) inviting applicants to join and be trained to become electronics engineers. It dawned on me that if I joined the RN I might be able to learn a trade, not necessarily become an electronics engineer, but any trade would be better than labouring for the rest of my working life. Furthermore, it would solve my lodgings problem by providing me with free accommodation.

I went to a Royal Navy recruitment office in Birmingham and there were three servicemen in smart uniforms interviewing candidates. After going through some routine questions, one of them asked me why I wanted to join the Royal Navy. I said that I wanted to learn a trade, and when they asked which trade, I brazenly said:

"I want to become an Electronics Engineer".

After they had picked themselves up off the floor from laughing, one of them said:

"You left school at 16. You have no educational qualifications. You are working as a labourer in a factory. Well Paddy, I need to inform you that you have no possibility of becoming an electronics engineer in the Royal Navy. You will probably be scrubbing decks or helping out in the galley (kitchen) for nine years (the minimum signing on period). Are you prepared to do that?"

I replied: "Yes, I'm ok with that."

A few weeks later I received a letter informing me that my application to join the Royal Navy had been approved. The letter contained train and bus passes and on 10 January 1966 I was to make my way to Cornwell where I would be collected and taken to HMS Raleigh, the R.N. training centre for new recruits.

"The Runner"

However, I needed to do one thing first, and that was to go back to Ireland to visit my mother.

I made my way to Pearl's house to call in on her and she told me that my mother wasn't well and that I shouldn't expect to see her as I remembered her. I travelled to Ballinasloe by bus and went to St. Brigid's Hospital. A female nurse took me to a small room where my mother was waiting. When I entered the room my mother looked at me somewhat furtively and then looked away. Nothing could have prepared me for the shock that I experienced on seeing her. What I saw was a small plump grey haired toothless old woman who was barely recognisable as my mother. She was standing by a wall but moving with a slight rocking motion, zombie like. She was 55 years old but looked more like 105.

I said: "Hello, mum", but she immediately diverted her gaze to the floor. I moved closer but she started to move away as if she was afraid of me.

I said: "Mum, it's me, Patsy. Don't you recognise me?"

She mumbled the name "Patsy" as if trying to make sense of it but she clearly didn't know me. I assumed that she was heavily sedated and I asked the nurse if that was the case. She said that my mother was on medication and that this was her normal everyday state. My mother started to mutter something barely audible, so I slowly moved closer and heard her say, "Cigarette. Cigarette."

I was smoking at that time so I offered her a cigarette from my packet of twenty. She took the entire packet and put it in her apron pocket without saying a word. For me it constituted a trivial gift that might bring her some comfort. My emotions went from shock to sadness to grief and then to a powerful sense of anger, but I couldn't vent my anger on anyone or anything and I felt totally helpless. I sat down and stayed for about 15 minutes during which time I mentioned the names, Val, Pearl, Ethel,

"The Runner"

Dennis in the hope that she would respond to them. She repeated some of the names, again as if trying to make sense of them, but she couldn't.

I wished I could have hugged her the way she hugged me when I was seven years old, but it was obvious that she did not want me to approach her and I had to respect that.

Prior to the visit I had been warned by Val and by Pearl that my mother would not be the person I remembered. That visit forced me to accept that my mother was gone and that she would never come back. However, despite what I saw on that visit, my overriding vision of my mother is that of the young, animated woman who came to visit Val and me in St. Joseph's. Thankfully, my enduring image of her is as reflected in the following photo.

Rose Ann Ward

(During the period that I was writing this book I happened to have a conversation with a friend when St. Brigid's hospital came up

during our conversation and he mentioned that many of the people who went into St. Brigid's never came out of it alive. How right he was and how was he to know that my mother was one of those unfortunate people. He may well be shocked if he reads this book.)

Royal Navy
I was both nervous and excited at the prospect of joining the Royal Navy. I felt that this would make a massive change to my life and I wondered if it would be for the better or turn out to be a terrible mistake on my part. I was still riddled with a lack of confidence in myself and self-doubt, but I knew I needed to find a way to leave my past behind and hope for a better future.

I had decided that I would be called Pat henceforth rather than Patsy (which was kept for my family). As I was writing this book I reflected on that period and this poem evolved in my mind and conveys my feelings at that time.

Leave The Past Behind
Leave the past behind but don't deny
A childhood that you could decry
If feeling awkward, shy, unsure
Face life's challenges and endure
Reach up, reach up to the sky
It's better to fail than fail to try
Face your fears, be the best you can
Come through this trial and be a man

The Navy had sent me travel passes that allowed me to catch buses and trains to make my way from Rugeley to HMS Raleigh in Plymouth. On 10 Jan 1966, aged 18, I started out on my odyssey into the unknown. When I arrived at Torpoint a RN bus was waiting to collect recruits and take us to HMS Raleigh, the RN training establishment. I was one of about 30 recruits to arrive

"The Runner"

that morning. With what seemed like undue haste we were all sent for a medical check. Some recruits failed the medical check-up and were bussed back to Torpoint to make their way home. I was 5' 6" tall and weighed exactly 123 lbs, which made it very easy to remember. That is the equivalent of 8 stone 11 lbs, or 55.8 Kg. Within six months I would weigh 132lbs. due to having three meals a day and a lot of exercise that would bulk me up a little.

There is a tradition in the Navy to assign nicknames where possible and I was called "Sharkey" because my surname was Ward. I never found out why all Wards were called Sharkey, but I liked the nickname because it gave me an immediate sense of belonging. Other nicknames were "Smudge" for "Smith", "Chalky" for "White", "Taff" for Welshmen, "Jock" for "Scots", etc. One unfortunate recruit was called "Dragarse" because his name was "Longbottom". Our group of recruits had come from all parts of the British Isles speaking with a wide range of accents. For the first time since moving to England I became less sensitive about my Irish accent and I seemed to meld into this new environment. We were scheduled to stay at HMS Raleigh for eight weeks during which time we would undergo military and physical training. There was a lot of marching and drilling with rifles, and a lot of cross country running. Some of the recruits struggled to cope with the physical demands, but I was surprised at how well I coped. Maybe my slim build was an advantage. We spent one weekend camping and trekking over a mountain. All of that physical activity was primarily intended to weed out weak recruits, and those who were unable to cope were sent home. I desperately needed the Navy at that time and I was determined to pass every test thrown at me.

There was a requirement for all recruits to pass a swimming test before we could leave HMS Raleigh. This required us to put on a boiler suit and heavy boots and jump off a 20-foot-high diving board into the deep end of a pool and then swim to the other end. We stood in a line at the top of the diving tower and inched

"The Runner"

forward as one by one a recruit was ordered to dive off the board into the water. Sailors stood on either side of the pool with long poles fitted with hooks so that they could pull out anyone in distress from the water. My turn came and I dived into the water. I was shocked when I instantly starting to sink to the bottom of the pool like a sack of potatoes. I thrashed at the water in a desperate attempt to stay afloat, but the water-soaked boiler suit restricted my movements and the dead weight of the boots pulled me down. Suddenly I felt a hook under my armpit and I realised it was the rescue pole. I tried to climb up the pole in panic but that was unnecessary as the experienced sailor pulled me to the surface and brought me safely to the side and up and out of the pool. The failed swimmers were then told that they would have to go for swimming lessons every morning at 6.30am until they passed the swimming test or risk being sent home. The following morning the failed swimmers turned up at the pool and we met our swimming instructor. He explained something interesting about our failed tests. He said that when people fall into water, their first instinct is to panic and thrash about in the water in an attempt to stay afloat, but they simply expend valuable energy in that futile exercise and invariably sink. He told us that we would repeat the diving board test immediately, but that this time we were to keep our arms by our sides as we entered the water. We were to allow ourselves to sink in the water until we hit the bottom of the pool or until our body buoyancy stopped the downward trajectory and brought us back to the surface. Dressed once again in a boiler suit and boots, I duly arrived at the top of the diving board. I jumped off the board and held my body and arms rigid. Sure enough I sank rapidly, but I had to have faith in that instructor and I forced myself to suppress my fear and my instinct to resist my descent. Finally my feet hit the bottom of the pool. I flexed my knees and then straightened them to propel myself upwards. I was amazed when I shot up several feet out of the water like a dolphin, except that my ascent was far less elegant than a dolphin's. The rescue sailor held out the pole invitingly towards me. I grabbed it and he calmly pulled me out of

"The Runner"

the water. With that success under my belt I could move on to the swimming lessons and the subsequent swimming test which I happily passed two weeks later.

Over the following weeks we did tests involving firefighting, crawling through flooded tunnels, attempting to cross a river on a 15 feet high rope in full battle gear including a rifle, (most of us fell into the river), and more physical training exercises. There were times when I doubted my ability to come through all of the challenges successfully, but I just ploughed on with determination because quitting was not an option.

The final challenge was a gas mask exercise that involved cramming about 30 recruits with gas masks into a small windowless hut. Over a loudspeaker we were told to put on the gas masks. Suddenly the lights went out and we could then feel tear gas on our skin as we fumbled in the dark to put the masks on. Several recruits panicked and started to scream. Unbeknown to us, "snatchers" had been placed in the hut with us and they had torches to help them to identify the screamers. The "snatchers" dragged the panicking guys quickly towards the door and ejected them. Announcements told us to stay calm. A short while later we were told to slowly make our way towards the exit where an instructor pulled off our masks as we arrived a few feet short of the door. This was intended to expose us to the tear gas. We were told not to rub our eyes because that would just press tear gas into them and make the experience worse. We all emerged from the hut coughing and spluttering and trying desperately to resist the urge to rub our eyes.

I didn't realise it at the time, but all of the demanding exercises, training and stressful tests at HMS Raleigh were intended to not only get us physically fit, but also to teach us to manage fear and to not allow it to debilitate and prevent us from emerging successfully through life threatening situations. I would carry those lessons with me for the rest of my life.

"The Runner"

During the final week in HMS Raleigh I went into a hall with about 100 other recruits. We sat at desks and were handed a variety of aptitude and intelligence tests so that they could stream us for our Navy careers. On completion of the tests we were sorted into three rows, A, B and C based on the results of the tests. I was placed in row C. When some of the other guys in that row heard my Irish accent, one of them said,

"Jesus, we have a Paddy in our group. We're going to be scrubbing decks."

But, surprise, surprise, Group C was to be sent to HMS Collingwood, the Navy's Electrical Engineering establishment. I couldn't believe my luck. Once there I spent the first three weeks in classes to study Maths, English and Physics with the intention of securing "O" level passes in those three subjects so that I could qualify for training in the Electrical Engineering School. If I had failed to secure those "O" level passes, I would have been sent to a different training establishment to be trained in something else. I threw myself wholeheartedly into my studies and secured the grades. I owe a huge debt of gratitude to Brother Egan for sending me to the Tech in Galway and to Jack Mahon and the other teachers there for giving me the lessons that made those "O" level passes attainable.

I next attended classes in basic electronics and electricity. I was good at Maths and this helped me to make sense of formulae and the basic electrical principles involved. A couple of months later we sat exams with the intention of streaming us to specialise in electronics or electrical engineering. Amazingly, I found myself in the electronics stream and spent the next six months studying electronics. On completing the course I was given the title "REM1", Radio electrical mechanic – grade 1. I was bursting with pride when the badge was sewn on to the arm of my shirt.
All RN shore bases such as HMS Collingwood had a very tall ship's mast at the main entrance to the base. Certain flags would be

"The Runner"

flown to indicate various things like whether the captain was at the base, etc. One of the flags related to dress code of the day, and specifically when to wear a raincoat. One day I was walking across the parade ground and an officer stopped me and asked me why I was wearing a raincoat. I replied that it was raining. He pointed to the mast and said:

"That flag is not flying. Take off the raincoat!!"

I realised then that I would quickly have to get used to the idiosyncrasies of the Royal Navy.

During my time at HMS Collingwood I took up several sports such as rugby and jogging. I had never played chess before and a guy named Brian taught me how to play chess simply because he had no one to play with. Brian delighted in thrashing me at chess, and on numerous evenings after class he would say:

"C'mon Sharkey, set up the chess board so that I can give you another thrashing."

These games were played in our messdeck (living quarters) and some of the mess mates would initially watch with fascination as Brian and I played chess. However they gradually lost interest when I was being beaten so routinely. I found chess interesting and I didn't mind losing. Besides, I felt that I was learning with each session.

One evening Brian went through his usual routine and asked me to set up the chess board. I had been thinking more and more about the game and I began to sense how or why he was winning so easily, so I decided to play more defensively to make it a bit more difficult for him to win and at least make a decent match of it. The board was set up and Brian anticipated another effortless win, but after a few moves by each of us Brian realised that he was in a competitive match for once and he started to concentrate

"The Runner"

more on the game. I just dug in and moves that had previously led to victory for him were proving ineffective, and the harder he tried the more the game began to slip away from him. Finally I made a move and shouted out "Checkmate". The other guys in the messdeck were shocked when they heard me and several came running up to see if it was true. One of them then said:

"Well I don't believe it. Sharkey Ward just beat the chess grandmaster."

Brian was furious and he insisted that he had not been concentrating and that I had been lucky and he then set up the board again. Sadly for him I went on to beat him again. I then went on to win the third game at which point he said he was having an off day and that he would sort me out the next time we played.

We played several times again, but Brian never won another game against me. Those wins taught me that I had the ability to learn, and to learn quickly.

I went back to Rugeley occasionally on weekend breaks to visit Dennis, Ethel and Val. They were delighted that I was studying electronics and they were also delighted to finally see me filling out from the scrawny boy they had known since childhood. Without realising it, I was metamorphosising into manhood.

Christine and I met up during those visits, but the buzz was seeping out of our relationship. The end came when I told her that I was due to join HMS Albion for a 23-month overseas tour. In late 1966 she wrote to tell me that she had met someone else and she wished me well.

To some extent it could be argued that by joining the Navy I had gone back into an institution, but this was a vastly different type of institution. First of all I was there voluntarily, and most importantly this institution was characterised by its

"The Runner"

encouragement and its provision of opportunities for personal development and growth. I felt I could thrive in this environment.

HMS Albion

A few months later I was assigned to HMS Albion. This was a small aircraft carrier that had helicopters rather than fixed wing aircraft. She had a crew of about 700 sailors, and could also house an additional 700 royal marines who could be transported anywhere in the world. Pearl's husband Leo had served in the Irish merchant navy, and we wrote to each other regularly during my time on the Albion.

I was nervously excited about going to sea, especially for such a long period, but this was to be a continuation of my career and my personal development and I saw it very much in that light. I would stay on board HMS Albion for 23 months and see a lot of the world.

On the first day on board, I and three other REM1 ratings were told to go to the Radio Control Room. Waiting for us was a Chief Petty Officer (CPO) and four Petty Officers (PO). Each of the ratings would be assigned to a Petty Officer. We were asked a few questions by the CPO and my Irish accent drew some smiles. The CPO assigned each of us to a Petty Officer, and I was assigned to a PO named "Dixie" Dean. I had the immediate impression that Dixie felt he had drawn the short straw in having me assigned as his trainee and that he would have to carry me for the next two years. Over the following weeks and months he would use me like a "Gofor" because he didn't trust me to do anything that required a bit of skill or competence.

In May 1967 we sailed to Liverpool to take part in the Battle of the Atlantic celebrations. At that time the Navy was still able to muster a large fleet of active service ships. A huge numbers of sailors dressed in full uniform were taken ashore to take part

"The Runner"

in a parade through the city centre and I felt great pride in participating. We were allowed to stay ashore until 11.00pm that night to enjoy the festivities. I did a city tour with two of my friends from the ship and as the evening closed in on us we went to a pub where we met three girls. I say girls, but they were a little bit older than us. It all seemed like a rerun of the movie "On the Town". I loved the Liverpool accent which became more pronounced with every drink the girls had. After a few drinks in the pub the girls invited us back to one of their houses for more drinks. We sat in the living room, and although I was now twenty years old I was still relatively quiet in comparison to my two friends who were very gregarious. Suddenly one of the girls stood up and said, "I fancy the quiet one. Come with me Sharkey", and with that she took me by the hand and led me upstairs to a bedroom. She asked me how many girls I had been with and I said I hadn't been with any. She said, "Oh my God, you're a virgin. How lucky am I?".

She told me not to be nervous as she started to undress me, but I was clearly very nervous, so she decided to put me at ease by partially undressing herself first. We kissed and then lay on the bed. She was very slow and gentle with me which helped me to relax and let nature take its course. We then chatted for a while as we shared a cigarette and a drink. She asked me how it had been and I said that it had been wonderful and I thanked her. As we went downstairs the others emerged from two other rooms. We said our goodbyes and made our way back to the Albion. I knew I would never see that girl again, but I would be eternally grateful to her and I would be reminded of her every time I heard the song "Liverpool Lou". That song is about heartache, but in sharp contrast my "Liverpool Lou" made my heart soar.

The Albion set sail for the Mediterranean to visit Gibraltar, Malta and Corsica. This was all wonderfully exciting for me. A few months later we headed for Singapore and Hong Kong. The CRO

"The Runner"

was responsible for keeping all radio and radar fully functional and I started to get familiar with the equipment. The main communications room was like a scene from a movie with a flurry of activity of officers and radio operators all going about their business of communicating with London, Singapore, Hong Kong and even Australia. Dixie would be called on to deal with malfunctioning equipment and I would tag along like his inferior Gofor. On one occasion he was asked to repair a malfunctioning teleprinter, an electronic typewriter that can send, receive and print radio messages. There was a problem with the carriage return function and Dixie moved the teleprinter to a desk with some space to work on it. We had to work amidst the chatter and clatter of people and equipment and in dimmed lighting.

The teleprinter had a very tightly coiled clock type spring whose function was to pull the carriage back to the start position at the end of each line of printing. Dixie started by disconnecting the end of the spring from the carriage but suddenly the spring exploded into a tangled mess. He had to carefully recoil the spring and anchor it in the coiled state while he freed up the carriage. When he had done that he carefully took hold of the tip of the spring with a pair of pliers in an attempt to reconnected it to the carriage, but just as he got within a whisker of hooking the spring on to the carriage it slipped from his grasp and again exploded into a tangled mess. The recoiling of the spring was a very delicate and slow process that took several minutes to complete. This was followed by trapping the spring in the fully coiled state while he prepared to connect it to the carriage. He tried several times to hook the spring to the carriage but each time as he stretched the end of the spring to hook it on to the carriage it would slip from his grasp. By now he was getting seriously exasperated. Worse still, he had attracted an audience of operators who were fascinated by the spectacle of the coiled spring exploding into a tangled mess each time he tried to fit it. He said he needed a coffee break, but first he coiled up the spring one more time and

"The Runner"

left it in the anchored state intending to try to connect it after the coffee break.

Dixie told me to tidy up the tools etc. while he went off for his coffee. Although I was initially disappointed that I had not been invited to have a coffee I decided to use the time to stick my head into the teleprinter to see what was going on. After studying it for a while I felt sure that I could hook that spring to the carriage. I picked up the pliers and slowly and carefully stretched the spring towards the hook on the carriage. The eye of the spring was now tantalisingly close to the hook and with one more gentle stretch the spring would be on the carriage. I took a deep breath and raised the tip of the spring up above the hook, and just as I was about to place it on the hook the spring escaped from my grasp and exploded into a tangled mess. I was instantly panic stricken and I didn't know what to do. I had seen Dixie carefully recoil the spring but I wasn't sure I could do that and hide the evidence of my tampering. Just then Dixie came back into the room. He took one look at the untangled spring and he knew straight away that I had tried to hook the spring to the carriage. He was furious and turned to me and said:

"You made that mess. Now you deal with it".

With that he walked out of the room. I came close to pleading with him not to abandon me, but that would only have deepened my sense of humiliation. A minute or so after Dixie had left I started to calm down and I began to shift my attention to the belligerent spring. I slowly and carefully began to rewind it into its coiled state and then I hooked it to the anchor point just as Dixie had done before. I then paused and studied the spring, the tip of the spring, the carriage and the hook on the carriage. I told myself that there was no earthly reason why these could not be cojoined and work in harmony once again. I realised that when Dixie and I had previously stretched the spring towards the carriage, we used both hands to do so, but I also noticed that the spring rose upwards

"The Runner"

gradually from its centre as it was being stretched and that each explosion of release followed from that rising movement. I decided to use my left hand to keep downward pressure on the spring as I once again started to stretch it towards the carriage. The spring was very strong and I had barely enough strength in my right hand to stretch the spring to within reach of the carriage. I didn't have the strength to make it on the first attempt so I anchored the tip of the spring while I took a rest and reflected further on what was going on with the body of the spring. Once again I took hold of the spring with the pliers and started to stretch it with my right hand while using my left hand to keep downward pressure on the centre of the spring. The tip of the spring came closer and closer towards the hook on the carriage and then came the moment, that magic moment when I slipped the tip over the hook and everything remained stable. I quickly placed a cover over the spring, and then came the moment of truth. With an inner prayer I pressed a key and the carriage moved one step to the right. I pressed several more keys as the carriage continued on its way. As it approached the end of the travel I hit a few more keys and held my breath, and as if in a nonchalant gesture, the carriage returned smoothly to its start position.

The watching operators applauded me. One of the operators put the teleprinter through its paces and gave me his seal of approval:

"Well done Sharkey".

As I waited for Dixie to come back to the room I basked in the warm feeling that comes from success, something I would teach others to do over time. Dixie finally returned and went instinctively towards the teleprinter to pick up from where he had left off, but to his surprise the teleprinter was fully encased and operational. He was gobsmacked, and as he stood there in stunned silence a huge sense of pride swept over me. I would draw on that event to inspire me in the future whenever I had moments of self-doubt.

"The Runner"

(The above story may seem insignificant to the casual reader, but given my background and the baggage that I had carried from my childhood - my feeling of inferiority and my total lack of self-confidence - that incident had a huge impact on my sense of self-worth and what I could achieve if only I could believe in myself. My success in dealing with the problem of the teleprinter gave me affirmation that I could be more than just a Gofor. I could be a contributor, an achiever, if only I had the opportunity and believed in myself).

In fairness to Dixie, his attitude towards me changed after that incident. Over the followings weeks I sensed that he now saw me as an asset and no longer as dead weight, and he started to trust me to take on more jobs on my own. This gave my self-confidence a huge boost and I began to believe in myself, and I finally started to come out of my self-imposed shell. Dixie and I would form a good working relationship during the rest of our time on the Albion, and a year later he recommended me for promotion to Leading Radio Electrical Mechanic (LREM - equivalent to a corporal in the army).

In July 1967 the Biafran civil war broke out and the Albion was sent with a contingent of royal marines to assist in the evacuation of British personnel. Many of these were nurses and doctors and teachers. The constant flow of helicopters in and out of Biafra over a period of two weeks ensured the safe withdrawal of hundreds of civilians. They were then shipped to Gibraltar to be flown back to the UK.

In October 1967 Britain was in the final stages of withdrawing from Aden (South Yemen) which had to be completed by a date in November. Once again the Albion was sent to assist in the evacuation. However, this time I was part of a team that made several flights into Aden to provide technical support. We flew in Wessex helicopters with an open door. I was one of 16 personnel on board on my first flight, and unfortunately for me I was seated

"The Runner"

right next to the open door. I found that flight very scary and I couldn't wait to land. One of my mates who flew with me on that trip was "Polly" Pieman. When we landed, we were told to be alert for snipers who might be located on the nearby hills.
The whole experience was getting scarier by the minute. As we huddled on our hunkers waiting for instructions, "Polly" said:

"Sharkey, can I ask you a question?"

I said yes and assumed that it would be an obvious question like "Are you scared?". I had my answer ready, but Polly surprised me when he said:

"If we were captured by the Arabs and tortured, how long do you think you would hold out?"

I replied: "Jesus, Polly. What made you think of that? I don't know. I don't think I'm particularly brave but I would do my best to keep my mouth shut for as long as possible, but I suspect that I would crack fairly quickly. What about you?"

Polly looked at me with a near haunted look on his face and then said:

"Sharkey, they would have to give me pills to shut me up!"

He then roared out laughing.

HMS Albion was stationed off the coast of Aden for 68 days and civilians were being brought on board almost every day and then transferred to merchant ships for transporting back to the UK. It was understandable that during those ten weeks or so some of the crew would show signs of stress. It must have been stressful also for wives and girlfriends. It was not unusual for someone to get a letter from a girlfriend ending their relationship. We referred to these as "Dear John" letters, after the 1960 song of

"The Runner"

the same name by Pat Boone. Rather than brood in silence, sailors were encouraged to pin their "Dear John" letter up on a notice board so that they could be consoled by their mates. The crew received a ration of two cans of beer each day, but most people hoarded a few cans in their lockers so that they could drink 4 or 5 cans on off duty occasions. Consoling the victim of a "Dear John" letter often involved gifting him a few cans of beer so that he could get drunk and drown his sorrows.

On one occasion a guy in our mess named Jones pinned up a "Dear John" letter on the board. Sympathy poured in from every direction and that evening cans of beer also poured in and Jones soon got drunk. He was getting close to passing out so it was decided to get him into his bunk. As his mates started to undress him and console him he started to mumble that he didn't have a girlfriend. One of his mates replied:

"Yes, Jones, you don't have a girlfriend anymore."

"No" replied Jones in his drunken stupor. "I – I – I never had a girlfriend. I was lonely and wanted you guys to feel sorry for me."

Suddenly an avalanche of pillows went flying at Jones and a couple of guys started to pulverise him with pillows. Jones was looking very sheepish the following morning, and his pain would last a while until he had repaid the gifted cans of beer.

The Aden experience was the nearest I ever came to seeing military action, and I was certainly relieved not to see it.

In 1968 we made a courtesy visit to Durban in South Africa. As we were approaching the harbour the Captain called for attention while he made an announcement.

"We will be docking in Durban within the hour and we will be here for one week. Remember that you are representing the

"The Runner"

Royal Navy and you must be on your best behaviour at all times. Now, there are three DON'Ts that you need to be aware of.

1. Don't drink the locally produced spirit called Cane wine. It is illegal and highly potent.
2. Don't go with the local women. Most of them have sexually transmitted diseases.
3. Don't talk politics. You may abhor apartheid but we are guests here and we do not question their rules".

He then made one final statement which surprised us.

"Because of the apartheid rule, all coloured crew members must use the rear gangplank to go ashore and all other crew members must use the forward gangplank. Coloured crew members must not mix with white crew members while ashore."

This came as a big shock to me because my best friend on board was "Rip" Kirby, who had Nigerian parents. Rip and I looked at each other in disappointment, but we would have to accept the ruling.

As we docked, a group of about thirty coloured South African men and women were gathered at the rear gangplank to welcome our coloured crew members ashore and arranged to take them away in buses to their townships. We had another coloured crew member called Dennis, and I didn't feel so bad for Rip when I saw that welcome party and the smile on his face as he and Dennis strolled down the gangplank to meet their hosts.

It was the hot season and we were dressed in our white tropical uniforms. I went ashore with several lads and we headed for the nearest bar. When we got there we ordered Cane wine. Several African girls came up to us and asked us to buy them a drink. We duly obliged and I remember putting my arm around one of the girls, taking a big swig of the Cane wine and saying:

"The Runner"

"Well, what do you think of apartheid?"

That was the last thing I remember about Durban because the Cane wine knocked me out and the next morning I woke up in cells on the Albion. Later that day I was put on charge and had to face the Captain. I stood to attention as the charge was read out.

"REM1 Ward was arrested by the local police when he was found at a major junction directing traffic. He was brought on board in a state of drunkenness and detained in the cells overnight."

The Captain said: "How do you plead, Ward?"

I had been assigned a lieutenant who was to act as my defence attorney. He leaned over to me and whispered to me:

"Guilty"

At this stage I was just robotic and I spluttered out:

"Guilty, Sir"

My punishment was all leave cancelled and extra duties every day for seven days. I had to ask my mates to get me some postcards of Durban and I started filling these in for posting home to Val, Ethel, Dennis and Leo/Pearl.

"Having a wonderful time here in Durban. It's a fabulous place. You should see all the wild animals. The people are very friendly and welcoming. I hope to come back here one day."

I never saw a wild animal, but at least the bit about the people being friendly was true.
Rip Kirby came back on board the night before we left Durban, but Dennis didn't. Rip told me that they had had a wonderful time in a village outside Durban where they were treated to native

"The Runner"

dancing and singing and traditional food and plenty of drink. He then told me that Dennis had decided to stay in Durban.

I told Rip about my misadventure and he said, "Sharkey, you should have put some boot polish on your face and come down the rear gangplank with me."

If only I could have.

I had sprained my wrist on the night before we sailed out of Durban and I went to the sickbay the following morning. I was amazed to see a long queue outside the sickbay. A male nurse dealt with sailors with minor injuries, and a doctor dealt with more serious problems that might require medication. As I was being treated by the nurse I could hear the doctor talking to a patient behind a screen. The doctor had a very loud voice and we could hear most of what he was saying to the patient.

"Well, what's wrong with you, lad?"

The guy replied something in a whisper.

Doctor: "Speak up, man, speak up. I can't hear a word you're saying."

The sailor replied in a barely audible voice, and the doctor replied:

"You have an itch. Where have you got this itch?"
The sailor again replied in a barely audible voice and the doctor bellowed.

"You have an itch down below. Let me see now. Is it your toe?"

"No, sir."
Doctor: "Is it your ankle?"

"No sir"

"The Runner"

Doctor: "Is it your knee. Am I getting warmer by any chance? Tell me outright. Do you have an itchy penis?"

The poor sailor was highly embarrassed at this stage as the doctor examined him.

Doctor: "Didn't the captain tell you not to go with the local women?"

He asked the guy to bend over and gave him an injection of penicillin in the buttock.

When I went back out I noticed that the queue had shrunk and it seemed that several sailors had left the queue, probably with the intention of coming back later when there would be fewer people present to hear their stories.

Getting drunk and being carried back on board that first night in Durban probably saved me from getting the Durban itch.

One interesting thing about the Albion was the wide range of accents. It was standard practice on the Albion to get new REMs to make public announcements on the Tannoy system, and regional accents would sound magnified by the Tannoy. The REM would be based in the Communications room and work 8-hour shifts for a month. The announcements to be made were always submitted in written form and then read out by the REM. Many of us thought it was very funny hearing announcements being made with a Welsh, Geordie or a Scottish accent. However, the smile was wiped from my face when I was notified that I had been rostered to make the Tannoy announcements for a month. I still had a strong Irish accent, but my bigger concern was that I couldn't correctly pronounce words beginning with "th", so "three" would be pronounced as "tree", etc. Initially I was being slagged for my brogue, but something odd started to happen when I started to receive an increasing number of messages that contained words beginning with "th", e.g.

"The Runner"

"De flight deck will be closed for "tree" hours from "tree-turty on Tursday".

I was getting slagged from all quarters about my inability to pronounce words with "th" and I set about addressing the problem. I started by listening carefully to how people pronounced those words and I took time in the evenings to lock myself away somewhere and read out loud. By the end of my month of duty as an announcer I had overcome my affliction and I could happily say:

"There are thirty-three thousand feathers on a thrush's throat."

Inspiration can come from unexpected sources
I was sharing a messdeck (sleeping quarters) with about 50 other sailors, and unfortunately there was one guy who was constantly baiting me. His name was Geordie, and whenever he had a couple of beers he would mouth off about my being from the Republic of Ireland and a supporter of the IRA and other nonsense. We both had the same rank of REM1. One morning he jumped out of his bunk and shouted at me:

"Sharkey, I'm going to study for the exam for promotion and when I'm promoted to LREM I'm going to make your life hell."
I thought he was bluffing initially, but his threat became a distinct possibility when he started locking himself away to study for a couple of hours in the evenings. I thought about this for a few days and then decided that there was only one option open to me, and that was to also study for the same exam. It would take about six months of study to be ready to take the exam and both of us went our separate ways each evening to study. This went on week after week. If I didn't understand something I was studying I would ask Dixie to explain it to me. He always helped and encouraged me. After about two months Geordie stopped studying and reverted to drinking his evening beers, but I continued studying. A few months later I sat and passed the exam and several weeks later I was promoted to "Acting LREM". I made

"The Runner"

a point of thanking Geordie for the inspiration to study for the promotion. I was now senior to him and I reminded him that it was a chargeable offence to insult anyone of a senior rank to yourself. The jibes stopped.

My tour on the Albion finished in 1969 and I went back to HMS Collingwood for further training in electronics and I was confirmed in the rank of LREM shortly after that.

I met my future wife in early 1969 and we were married later that year. We moved into a Navy married quarters near HMS Collingwood and our son Paul was born in 1970.

Sport had become a big part of my life in the Navy where I took up rugby, soccer and squash, and I even represented HMS Collingwood in a chess competition. I had hated cricket all my life, but one day I was drafted in to make up a cricket team. I was surprised at how much I enjoyed playing it as opposed to just watching it, and that experience certainly changed my opinion about cricket.

I was very fit and I took to squash like a duck to water and started to feature in competitions. I entered a knockout competition for the Collingwood cup and found myself progressing with ease initially and I began to fancy my chances of winning the cup. I was delighted when I was drawn against a Commander in the semi-final and I was already looking at the other side of the draw to see who my likely opponent in would be the final. Just before the start time for our match the Commander turned up wearing baggy oversized shorts and an oversized tee shirt. He was probably aged about fifty and I couldn't help but smile to myself. This was a five-set match. The first set went to the wire but he won it 9-8.

He asked me if I would like a short break and I assumed that he was tiring so I said no and off we went straight into the second set. To my surprise he won that set 9-6. He again suggested that

"The Runner"

we have a short break but I assumed that he was just trying to get his breath, so I told him to play on. He won that set 9-5. I was out of the competition and he progressed to the final. I felt numb and started to wonder why the match had gone so badly wrong for me. When we stepped out of the court and sat down to cool off he turned to me and said:

"Now young man. I have a word of advice to give you. You are very young and fit, but did you notice that I had you running around that court like a hare whereas I did hardly any running. It was easy to beat you because you rely entirely on your fitness to win matches. If you ever learn to play squash with your brain instead of your legs you will become a much better player."

Despite my disappointment, I knew that he was right, and I decided to put that advice to good use.

When I finished the electronics course in 1971 I was assigned to the Ratings Control Office (RCO) at HMS Collingwood while waiting for a posting to my next ship. A Chief Petty Officer named George ran the RCO and he had the responsibility of assigning sailors to their next posting, either a surface ship or a submarine. I certainly did not fancy being posted to a submarine. Although George was two ranks more senior to me we struck up a friendship and most Monday mornings I would call into George's office and ask him how his weekend had gone. George loved the Navy but he was nearing age 55 when he would have to retire. George would talk about his wife and their grown-up children and his rose garden. I mentioned that we had just had our first baby, a boy name Paul. My son Paul was suffering from respiratory problems at that time and the doctor who was treating him said that Paul would have to live with those problems throughout his life. The reason for Paul's problem was that there was no central heating in our married quarters and the walls and windows dripped with condensation. I mentioned Paul's problem to George and he would often enquire about him.

"The Runner"

Some of the staff in the RCO were WRNS (Women's Royal Navy Service) and they did most of the secretarial work. They would type up the duty roster every week and it would be posted on the main notice board with the ratings names in alphabetical order. Night patrols around key installations at Collingwood were the least popular duty, and the worst of those was from midnight till 4.00am. In general, ratings could expect to get rostered for that duty about once every 4 – 5 weeks. One week a rating named Whitehead got that duty, but he was very unlucky to get the same duty again two weeks later. He came into the RCO and complained bitterly to the WRNS (pronounced "wren") who had typed up the roster even though she had no say in the rostering. He was quickly told to shut up and get out. The WRNS was clearly upset at the verbal assault. The following week Whitehead went to check the roster and he was relieved when his name didn't appear opposite the 12.00 – 4.00am shift. He was even more surprised when he couldn't find his name at all so he went to the RCO to check up on why he hadn't been rostered. He went to the same WRNS, but this time with a more civil manner. She told him that he had definitely been rostered so they went down through the list together. Suddenly she gasped and said:

"Oh my God, I'm so sorry. I've misspelled your name. I typed an S where the W should be."

Whitehead never complained about a duty again.

After about two months working in the RCO I was called one day to George's office. Unusually he asked me to close the door behind me and then asked me to sit down. He said he had a posting for me and that he would be sorry to see me go. I had mixed feelings about going back to sea, but I knew I would have to accept any posting given to me. George asked me about Paul and I said he was as well as could be expected. He then said that maybe what he needed to get over his bronchitis was a warmer climate.

"The Runner"

I nodded in agreement and said that there was no chance of that happening. George then looked at me and said,

"Sharkey, I have two postings and I will let you choose the one you want. You can join a destroyer and go to sea for nine months, or you can go to Singapore with your wife and son for a shore-based posting for 24 months. Which will it be?"

I was shocked and asked him if he was serious about Singapore. He said "Yes, but keep your voice down otherwise I will have a stampede outside my door."

I said I would love to take up the Singapore posting and he told me to get ready to leave within four weeks. Within a few months of arriving in Singapore, Paul's respiratory problems had completely cleared up and it never bothered him again. George was correct when he said that all Paul needed was a warm climate, and Paul and I are hugely indebted to George.

I was based at the Naval base near Sembawang village in Singapore and was attached to a group called ANZUK, comprising of personnel from the Army, Navy and Air Force of Australia, New Zealand and the UK. We worked in the Communications centre maintaining and operating the radio equipment. It was strange initially to be in my Navy uniform working with guys in their Army or Air Force uniforms. We worked in shifts and I worked mainly with a New Zealand Army guy named Bill. We have kept in touch ever since those days in Singapore and I have visited Bill in New Zealand and he has visited me in Ireland.

The Communications centre comprised transmitters and receivers for radio traffic and was a hub for communications between various places such as London, Hong Kong, Manila and Canberra, etc. Our job was to maintain the equipment and keep it operating 24/7 throughout the year.

"The Runner"

I was promoted to Petty Officer during my time in Singapore and I was assigned to take over management of the teleprinter workshop. This was a large workshop with about 40 technicians working full time repairing and servicing teleprinters. The workforce comprised of Chinese, Indians and Malaysians, and I was the only Western guy in the workshop. It was amazing how harmoniously those people worked together and I never saw a single disagreement between them. Most of the time I had to help the technicians with technical problems, but occasionally I had to deal with other problems such as sickness, absenteeism or family issues. Little did I know that this was in effect my training for a future career in management.

Our daughter Kerry was born in Singapore in October 1972 and I was given a few days leave to help my wife with her recovery, etc. A day or two after the birth I was given a birth certificate for Kerry and I had to go to the workshop to deal with an urgent problem and I happened to leave the birth certificate on my desk. The following Monday I returned for full time work. When I entered the workshop I was surprised to see all of the technicians standing waiting for me to enter. I got a big round of applause, and just as I was about to thank them one of the Chinese technicians stepped forward with a teddy bear as a gift for Kerry.

His name was Kim Seng. (It's strange how some names stick in your mind forever). Kim Seng handed me the gift and I thanked him, and then he surprised me when he said that he needed to explain something. I was puzzled at this, but then he went on to remind me that I had left Kerry's birth certificate on my desk. That evening as he was finishing work he looked at the certificate and copied some of the numbers from it. On his way home he bought a lottery ticket and used the numbers from Kerry's certificate as his entry for the lottery. To his amazement he won a prize, not a massive prize, but a prize, nonetheless. He explained to me that in Chinese culture if you receive good luck from someone you must repay that luck otherwise it will become bad luck, and that was

"The Runner"

why he had bought the teddy bear, to share his good luck in choosing the winning numbers from Kerry's birth certificate.

To this day, I find that story utterly amazing.

At the end of my Singapore tour in 1973 I returned to HMS Collingwood to do a course in advanced electronics. I wished those recruiters in Birmingham could have seen me then: Petty Officer Ward – Electronics Engineer.

I made new friends during my time at HMS Collingwood, and I hooked up with three Welsh guys, Taff, John and Derwent. I suppose we got on well because we were all Celts. Whenever anyone was looking for Derwent I couldn't resist saying: "Derwent that way."

On one occasion the four of us had gone to a dance at HMS Collingwood with our wives, and when the music had finished for the night we started singing. At one stage the four of us were standing together in the middle of a cleared dance floor singing rugby songs. Suddenly Taff started singing the Welsh national anthem as if to bring the curtain down on the night. Before I knew it we had linked arms to make us a tight knit group and the other two guys joined in singing the Welsh national anthem. I was in a dilemma because I didn't know the words to the anthem. I could have broken from the group and walked off the dance floor and left them to it but I remembered some words from the chorus so I decided to bluff it out and mouth the other words as if I was singing them, and when the chorus arrived I wholeheartedly roared out the only two words that I remembered. We got a huge round of applause as we finished and walked off the dance floor and people started patting me on the back and saying: "Well done, Taff."
I suppose I became an honorary Welshman that night.

By now my friend George had long retired and I wondered where my next posting would take me. I was quite happy when it turned

"The Runner"

out to be HMS Hampshire, a destroyer. I was flown to Gibraltar to join her and as a Petty Officer I was assigned a young "Gofor". I remembered my days as a "Gofor" on HMS Albion. In contrast to my initial experience, I encouraged him as much as possible and he was a great help to me. I would like to think that he went on to become an Officer.

The Hampshire did a three-month tour of the Mediterranean and then had to go back to docks for upgrading with new equipment. I returned to HMS Collingwood for one last time. I signed on for an extra term so that I could finish a course that would qualify me for the rank of Chief Petty Officer. However, on completion of the course I reflected on the fact that Paul and Kerry were now six and four years old respectively and I reasoned that I couldn't be an absentee father going forward so I left the Navy in December 1976, almost eleven years to the date that I had signed up.

The number one song in the pop charts was "If you leave me now", by Chicago. Every time I heard it I wondered if I had made the right decision.

Return to Civvy Street
I went back to Rugeley in January 1977 and got a job as a Test Engineer with Thorn Automation. I was very unhappy there, not least because I missed the camaraderie of the Navy, but also because I found the work at Thorn unchallenging, repetitive and boring.

I was 30 years old and still quite fit and I had developed a love for rugby, so I joined the local rugby club. This enabled me to forge new friendships as well as compensating to some extent for my boring job.

Rugeley had three rugby teams and we played in the local Midlands league, playing teams in Cannock, Birmingham, and

"The Runner"

Wolverhampton, etc. I was asked to captain the Rugeley Seconds team which required me to organise playing kits and transport for our away matches. It was normal practice for some of the players to call into a pub on the way back to Rugeley. On one of those occasion we had two cars with eight players. I arranged to go into the pub alone and order the drinks and call out to the others when the drinks had been poured. I went to the bar and asked for one pint and seven half pints of beer. The barman looked at me askance but I explained that my mates were in the car park and that we had already had a beer in another pub and they didn't want to drink too much. As soon as the drinks were poured I put my had to my mouth and shouted out:

"Hi Ho", "Hi Ho", and with that my teammates came shuffling into the pub on their knees and singing the song from Snow White and the Seven Dwarfs:

"Hi Ho, Hi Ho, it's off to work we go………"

As they arrived at the bar I handed down the half pints to each of them. They then made their way to a table to consume the drinks. We got a great round of applause from the patrons and then ordered full pints.

In 1979 I saw an advertisement in an engineering magazine for engineers to join a USA company in Ballinasloe in Ireland. Up until then, I had no notions of ever going back to Ireland, but I was excited at the possibility of working for an American company. I applied for a job and was invited to Ireland for an interview. I got a job offer and returned to Ireland to start working with Square D Company in October 1979.

"The Runner"

Reflections

I am very grateful to the UK for enabling me to unshackle myself from my childhood in Ireland and to provide me with the space and time to start a new life.

I owe an immense debt to the Royal Navy. I joined as a naïve 18-year-old with little more than aspiration and hope. My siblings often said that I entered the Navy as a boy and emerged as a man. I fully agreed. The Navy developed me as a man and gave me self - confidence. I became a Petty Officer and a qualified electronics engineer, and I left the Navy with a huge sense of confidence in my ability to continue to develop and grow as a person. My advice to any young person who feels at a loss in life would be to consider joining the military where you will find stability, encouragement, opportunity and the space and time to develop and grow into the person you can be.

The stories about Brian (chess) Dixie Dean (the teleprinter), Geordie (promotion) and the Commander (Squash) when taken alone may seem little more than interesting, but each of these was a key step in my personal development. I am fascinated by how people we meet on the road of life can intentionally or unintentionally motivate us to do better. Each one of those people helped to push me further down that road and collectively they instilled in me greater confidence in my ability to advance further.

"The Runner"

Chapter 3 – Return to Ireland

I returned to live in Ireland in October 1979, and other than making a few trips to Dublin to visit Pearl I had not visited any other part of Ireland since the visit to my mother in 1965. Once again I found myself in a "strange" country. Ireland had changed a lot since my departure in 1963, but it was still quite introspective politically and socially and everything about it seemed alien to me. However, there was a feeling that radical change was coming, driven largely by membership of the EU and the resultant opening up of Ireland to new countries and to new ideas. Inward investment by US multinational companies would drive economic change, and EU membership would drive social change.

Square D was an American switchgear company manufacturing circuit breakers and related products. They set up a manufacturing facility in Ireland to gain access to EU and Middle East markets, and they benefitted from Ireland's low corporation tax rate.

I heard that there was a squash court in Garbally college so I went there one evening to see if I could get a game. Two guys had just finished a game and one of them left the squash court while the other guy remained there and just hit a few shots to keep himself warm. I asked him if he would like a game and he was delighted to accept. I joined him a few minutes later and we hit a few warmup shots and then got into a serious game. I was shocked when he started swearing at every poor shot he made or at every point that I won. I had never met anyone who had used such language during a squash match. I won three straight games easily which only added to his displeasure and his awful language and he left the court much displeased with himself. I was relieved when he left. The next day at work I told my fellow workers about the incident and they said that it was just an Irish thing to use bad language at every possible opportunity. The following Sunday I went to mass and I got the shock of my life when my foul-mouthed squash opponent turned out to be the priest serving mass. Having gotten over my initial shock I thought it was very funny when he turned to the congregation, smiled and said:

"Now please offer the sign of peace to those around you."

My initial position at Square D was as an automation engineer, helping to set up machines for the production and testing of circuit breakers. The automation work was completed after three years and I was then moved into product development. That's where I learned about Square D technology used in a special type of circuit breaker intended for electric shock protection. These products were known as Residual Current Devices, (RCDs – known as GFCIs in the USA), and Square D had state of the art technology for use in electronic RCDs. I found the design work particularly interesting.

In 1984 I began to have problems with my knees due to the stresses of squash. My GP sent me to Portiuncula hospital for some physio treatment. The department was run by a Sister Mary and she offered to treat me.

She started by using a machine for electrotherapy. This required her to stick a pad on my left thigh and rub a gel on my left knee and then rub a probe on my knee to stimulate the tissue with an electrical current. She would turn up the power until I could feel a strong tingling sensation in my knee. She would then repeat that process on my right knee.

The treatment was to take several sessions, and because we had both travelled a lot we got into long absorbing conversations about various countries during each session. On one occasion Sister Mary went through the standard routine of placing a pad on my left thigh and turning up the current to a tingling level and then rubbing the probe on my left knee to stimulate the tissue. On this occasion she was in full flow recounting a story about her time in Africa and without thinking she went around to the other side of the bed and put some gel on my right knee and started to

"The Runner"

rub the probe on that knee. She was surprised when I grabbed the probe to stop the treatment.

"What's wrong, Pat", she asked.

I replied: "Sister, you normally place the pad on my left thigh when you treat my left knee, and then you place the pad on my right thigh when treating my right knee, but this time you have left the pad on my left thigh and you are treating my right knee."

She replied: "Don't worry, Pat, the current will still get there."
I replied: "Yes, Sister, I know that. It's the path that the current is taking that's bothering me."

She gasped and ran out of the room with her hands clasped to her face. She came back a few minutes later blushing profusely, and then quietly and calmly moved the pad over to my right thigh and continued her conversation about Africa.

I was actually very happy at Square D. In doing the RCD design work one of my tasks was to test and evaluate competitor products from the UK. Most of the UK products seemed highly inferior to the Square D products and I realised that those companies were or would soon be in need of modern RCD technology because the use of RCDs was gradually increasing globally. I began to wonder if I could set up a company to provide that technology to switchgear companies, but all I seemed to do was ponder about it.

The thought of starting my own business welled in me throughout 1984 and I found it more and more difficult to shake it off. One evening I was watching TV and happened upon Shakespeare's play *"Julius Caesar"*. There was a scene in the play where Brutus was trying to urge his comrades to support him for a coming battle, and Brutus made the rallying call:

"The Runner"

"There comes a tide in the affairs of men which taken at the flood leads on to fortune."

In that moment I thought to myself – the RCD industry may be the tide that can lead me on to fortune, and if I fail to catch it now I will probably never get another chance. In December 1984 I decided to catch my tide and I gave my notice to leave Square D. It did not occur to me that I still retained much of my innate optimism which in this case was underpinned by naivete about how to set up and manage a business, and that I may well have hit a self-destruct button.

I needed a name for the business, and by playing around with my surname I came up with the company name of

Western Automation Research & Development
I was just lucky that my surname wasn't Shaughnessy or some other unwieldy name. For convenience I initially referred to the company as Western Automation. My first official day at WA was 5 January 1985, working from home.

My wife was working at Square D at that time and that gave us a steady source of income. My plan was to develop an electronic circuit that could be offered to OEM companies (Own Equipment Manufacturers) making RCDs for the electrical switchgear industry. However, development of a proven RCD design was expected to take about 12 months, so I needed to do something else in the meantime to try to generate some income to help fund the design work. I cashed in my pension fund which yielded about £3000. In parallel to trying to develop the RCD solution, my intention was to earn some money by providing electronic repair services to companies having equipment that needed servicing or calibrating.
My first venture outside my door was to the local branch of Bank of Ireland in Ballinasloe where I also had my personal account. When I asked to see the manager I was given an abrupt "WHY?".

"The Runner"

I replied: "I have left Square D to start my own business and I will need a bank account for my company so I would like to introduce myself to the manager."

The bank manager was not exactly on call back then and you normally had to make an appointment to see him, but I was naïve and simply asked to see him. (Female branch managers were as rare as hen's teeth in those days, but thankfully that is no longer the case.)

I was asked to take a seat in a waiting area, and eventually brought in to see the manager.

"Sir, this is Mr Ward. He would like to speak to you about his new business."

The manager asked me to take a seat, but I stood for a while without saying anything. He then said:

"Take a seat. Why don't you take a seat?".

I thought about it for a moment and then said:

"It might be disrespectful if I sit, but I'm not sure whether I should stand or kneel because I've just noticed that your initials spell **G O D**."

The manager's name was **G**eorge **O'D**ea, and he just laughed, and that was my first encounter with George. I sat down and told him about my plans for WA and he said he would be delighted to open an account and wished me well. I was required to give a personal guarantee in order to secure a line of credit. I didn't think twice about signing up for that.

The bank quickly abbreviated my company name to WARD, which annoyed me, so I decided to further abbreviate the name to WA because I didn't feel comfortable with WARD. I had visions of

"The Runner"

being introduced as, "This is Ward from WARD", and I certainly didn't want to endure that kind of introduction.

I needed several months to develop my own RCD circuit but in the meantime I needed to get a source of income, so I sent out letters to companies in the surrounding counties offering my services as an electronics service engineer. My first service job came from a company called General Tyre who asked me to repair and calibrate a machine for checking the pressure of tennis balls. General Tyre was obviously involved in the tyre industry and they somehow branched out to making tennis balls. Their tennis balls were used in Wimbledon and other major tennis tournaments around the world, and tournament tennis balls had to have a pressure within a certain band. Too low a pressure would make the ball sluggish and too high a pressure would make the ball too fast. The calibration machine worked on a very simple but clever principle of operation. A ball was placed in a holder exactly six feet above a metal plate and it would be dropped automatically. When it hit the plate it made a sound that was recorded. The ball would bounce vertically upwards and then drop to the plate a second time and the second impact on the plate was recorded. The interval between the two recordings was proportional to the air pressure in the ball. The interval between the two recorded sounds from the plate was measured in milliseconds, (mS).

A sluggish ball would not bounce very high and the interval between the two recordings would be short. A ball with high air pressure would bounce very high and the interval between recordings would be much longer. The balls were graded according to their responsiveness. The balls for tennis tournaments had a tight window of a few hundred milliseconds between bounces and were premium priced. Very sluggish balls were rejected, and the remainder were put on general sale.
I managed to repair and recalibrate the machine and submitted an invoice for my work. That was WA's first payment as a trading

"The Runner"

company and I now wish I had framed that cheque, but I needed the money and cashed it in.

I took on similar work with other companies just to generate some level of income. By the end of 1985 I had designed a circuit for use in an RCD and filed a patent application for it. However, the RCD needed a special component for its operation and that was supplied by Plessey Semiconductors based in Oldham, England. I was very doubtful that they would deal with a start-up company, but nonetheless I wrote to them and told them of my Square D connection. That seemed to open the door because they sent me an invitation to meet with them. I decided to buy a briefcase just to look a bit more professional. The briefcase had one of those dial type coded locks which was initially set to "0000", and with the new code correctly set you could slide a button sideways to open the briefcase. I set a new code on the lock, packed my documents into the briefcase and set off for Manchester airport. On arriving at Plessey I was taken into a fancy boardroom where there were several managers and engineers. After an introduction all round, I gave a brief explanation of my business plan. I then tried to open the briefcase but to my horror the slider wouldn't budge. I checked the code and it looked correct, but the lock wouldn't open. I set the briefcase on my lap and frantically rotated the dials and then brought them back to the code, but still the lock wouldn't open. At this stage I had a silent audience in the room staring at me and I could feel panic sweeping over me. I was racking my brain to make sure I had the correct code, but still no success. I then owned up and said I had just bought the briefcase the previous day and that I must have forgotten the code. I asked for a knife or a pair of scissors so that I could cut open the briefcase. There was shock in the room. One of the engineers volunteered to go and get a knife, and as he reached the door I set the dials to "0000" and to my amazement the briefcase popped open when I slid the button to the side.
I clearly had not changed the code properly. I sheepishly admitted my mistake, which was followed by laughter and relief – their

laughter and my relief. I could feel the tension go out of the room as we got down to discussing the technical details of my proposal.

Given the size of that company, I was pleasantly surprised at how Plessey responded to my request. The component I needed was called an ASIC and it was available at a good price, but it would take several months to develop it and get it ready for production. Enterprise Ireland (formerly The Industrial Development Authority of Ireland) is the government agency set up to support Irish industry and they provided me with financial support to offset some of my startup costs.

In late 1985 I wrote to six companies in the UK to inform them about WA and about my new RCD technology. They all responded positively to me and invited me to visit them. By now I was incurring more costs than my total income and WA was slipping into debt which was funded by bank borrowings. I visited the companies and demonstrated the technology, and they were all impressed. However, I was shocked at the proposed timeframes of 1 – 2 years for the first five companies to adopt my technology and I knew that WA could not survive for another year without sales of the RCD technology. The sixth company I visited was relatively new to the industry and needed modern RCD technology to make a breakthrough. Instead of sensing and exploiting their need I focused almost entirely on my need to generate sales, and from a position of weakness I signed a highly unfavourable Supply Agreement. The customer promised sales of about £750,000 per year, but the Agreement stipulated that WA could not supply the technology to any other company. I would soon regret signing that contract.

WA had no manufacturing facility and I urgently needed to find a subcontract manufacturer. I found a subcontractor in Cork and we got initial production flowing in June 1986. This generated sales and cash flow that relieved pressure from the bank. However, the subcontractor had larger customers than WA and in the lead up to

"The Runner"

Christmas demand from other customers increased to the point that they had insufficient capacity to continue production of the WA product. I suddenly had a crisis on my hands where I had a customer demanding deliveries that I couldn't meet, a resultant drop in income, and suppliers demanding to be paid. I tried another subcontractor, but they also turned out to be unreliable and in late 1986 I decided that I needed to acquire a building somewhere so that WA could take over manufacturing of our product. I was very fortunate to find an old store in Ballinasloe that I could convert for manufacturing. The building was over 200 years old and in a sorry state, so my first job was to get the place cleaned up and ready for assembly of our electronic RCD technology.

Unemployment was at a very high level in Ireland at that time, so I had no difficulty in recruiting people. My next task was to train them in electronic assembly. I bought second hand production equipment and when production started in early 1987 I was relieved to see our finished product coming off our own assembly line for the first time. The setbacks with the subcontractors had cost us dearly to the extent that we were currently operating at a loss, but the grants from EI were keeping us afloat and the expectation was that cash flow would improve after a stuttering start.

"The Runner"

**1986 – Our First Home
Bridge Street, Ballinasloe**

Bridge Street Interior

One day in 1987 I went to my family doctor with terrible pain in my face and neck, and he said I had had an attack of shingles. He reckoned it was stress related and asked me if I had any hobbies. I told him I had no hobby since giving up playing squash

"The Runner"

a few years earlier. He suggested that I take up playing bridge for the winter and golf for the summer. I decided I would initially go for bridge lessons and I was soon raring to play bridge. I had no bridge partner for a while, but a Sister Magdalene took me under her wing and we started playing bridge together. I was like a terrier chomping at the bit and I started making ridiculous bids and getting into deep trouble. Sister Magdalene was very patient with me, but on one occasion I saw her raise her eyes towards the ceiling and her lips were moving as if praying. I think she said something like:

"Lord, forgive him for he knows not what he's doing."

I began to curb my aggressive play and over the following 25 years Sister Magdalene and I went on to become a formidable partnership, winning several tournaments together.

I decided to take up golf in the summer of 1987. WA was heavily in debt at that time and I didn't have the money to buy golf clubs from a golf shop. I noticed an advertisement in a newspaper for a half set of clubs for £49.00 including a golf bag and delivery, a real bargain if ever I saw one, so I sent a cheque in the post and the clubs duly arrived about a week later. They looked nice and shiny and they included a booklet with golf tips. I bought a carton of three golf balls and went to Ballinasloe golf club the next evening and paid a green fee for a round of golf. My heart was racing at the prospect of my first round of golf. I watched some guys on the first tee box as each of them took out a driver and teed up a golf ball. Swoosh went the driver, and the ball went sailing down the fairway in each case. A piece of cake.

I was on my own and next to go. There were two other guys waiting for me to tee off. I stepped up on to the tee box and teed up the ball just like those guys did earlier on. I took a couple of practice swings, and then swoosh went the club - and missed the

"The Runner"

ball! I took two more swings and missed each time. One guy turned to the other and said:
"He has a nice swing, hasn't he?"

The other guy replied: "Yes, but I wish he would just hit the ball and move on".

I turned to them and said: "I'm trying to hit the ball but I keep missing it."

They burst out laughing. I discovered then that you get little sympathy in golf. I stepped down off the tee box somewhat embarrassed and told them to go ahead. I watched enviously as the two guys hit great drives straight down the fairway.
I ventured back on the tee box thinking that all I had to do was focus on the ball. I teed up the ball and glued my eyes to it. Swoosh went the club and I struck the ball with a ferocious blow. The ball went flying off down the fairway, and the club head flew somewhere else because I was left standing there with just the shaft of my driver in my hands. So much for my bargain set of golf clubs. I hacked my way around the first five holes, at which point I had run out of golf balls, my entire stock of three balls now lying in impenetrable jungle out there somewhere. As I walked back to the clubhouse feeling somewhat disappointed I felt that despite the loss of the club head and my three golf balls it had been an enjoyable experience. I decided to go into the clubhouse and have a beer to drown my sorrows but when I went to the bar to order a beer I saw the head of my golf club sitting on the bar with a sign next to it:

"Would the owner please collect".
My humiliation was complete as I took the driver head and threw it in a bin and went home swearing never to play that damn game again, but a few days later I was back at the golf course because I now had the golf bug. I put my misfortune down to my clubs and

sought out a replacement set. I managed to buy a used half set of clubs and thus began my golfing odyssey.

I am indebted to my GP for giving me the best prescription I ever received from any doctor – a dose of bridge and a dose of golf to be taken liberally throughout one's life.

A Sinking Feeling
I knew very little about finances and cash management at that time but I was about to get a crash course in basic business finance. The first set of accounts for WA was produced in early 1988 and even with my limited understanding of financial statements I could see that we were in serious trouble.

Total sales to date had been IR£325,000 with a loss of IR£66,118. We had an overdraft of about IR£12,000, and no cash.

I was a busy fool who was going broke.

It was now apparent that the level of sales was nowhere near the expected figure and the contract price left us with a tiny profit margin at best, and because of the initial setbacks with subcontractors we were in serious debt with no obvious way to clear it quickly. I had to accept that my inexperience in running a business had led to this state. I was learning on the job, but it was questionable as to whether or not I would acquire sufficient management know-how quickly enough to keep the company afloat.

I managed to achieve some cost reductions and by about May 1988 I felt that WA had reached a turning point in that it was finally trading profitably on a day-to-day basis. However, in June 1988 I received a bolt from the blue when the customer phoned to inform me that that they had fallen into a big hole and that

"The Runner"

they wanted no more products from WA. The caller, who worked in the purchasing department, didn't want to engage in any protracted conversation with me and abruptly hung up. I may have missed some of the earlier bits of the conversation because I was in a state of shock, numb of mind and body, but slowly and inexorably I began to realise the scale of the problem facing me. WA now had no customer and a pile of debt. The company was insolvent and I had a personal guarantee on the line which could result in the forced sale of my house. In that moment I found myself in that place that all entrepreneurs fear, the moment when you realise that everything you have worked so hard for is about to be swept away.

I looked out at our production area. We had twenty people employed and I didn't know how I was going to give them the news that I had to let them go. The following morning I called the customer's financial director. I was surprised when he took my call. He explained that there was an apparent defect in their product that had resulted in cancellation of orders from their customers. I sympathised with him and asked that they formally terminate the contract so that I could try to find replacement customers for our technology. He said that they wouldn't do that, and he left WA for dead.

I informed the bank of the situation, and our credit facility was immediately withdrawn. Cheques could now only be issued if there were funds available to cover them. I let all of the employees go except my production supervisor. The situation for WA was now dire. Whilst reflecting on the scale of the problem facing WA, my Royal Navy training started to kick in. Most failures should be seen as just setbacks rather than total failure, so in most cases we should use the word "falter" rather than "failure". When we think of faltering we generally assume that we can get up and try again and in doing so we sustain the possibility of achieving success.

"The Runner"

**"When Sense And Reason Scream at you to GIVE UP,
Hope Quietly Whispers - TRY AGAIN"**

I had to believe that I would find a way to save WA and I acted in that vein.

The customer owed WA money but it was obvious that would not be forthcoming. WA had liabilities of about IR£160,000, and thanks largely to generous grants from EI we had just over IR£100,000 in cash at the bank. Could that be our lifeline? Over the following few days I arranged to fly to Manchester to visit our biggest creditor, Plessey, and I also arranged to visit a legal firm in England on that trip. I duly arrived at Plessey, this time without a briefcase. They were shocked when I gave them the news about the customer, and even more so when I told them that I couldn't pay them, at least not straight away. They asked me why I had bothered to visit them if I couldn't pay them.
I explained that there were several companies in the UK who wanted to buy our technology, and now that the relationship with the current customer had ended WA was free to offer the technology to other companies. I pointed out that Plessey was our biggest creditor and I asked them to give me a letter stating that they were willing to give me 12 months to get the company back on its feet. I in turn would give a commitment that if any other creditor took WA to court over non-payment I would immediately discharge our debt to Plessey. One of the managers asked me what book I got that idea from, and I said, "I just thought of it, and I had to come here and try to persuade you to give me that breathing space."

They smiled at each other, and one said, "I have to admire your nerve. We will have to talk to the credit department, so we can't make any commitments now."

"The Runner"

I had had a very good relationship with Plessey ever since that first meeting when I couldn't open my briefcase, and I felt optimistic that Plessey would give me that breathing space. As I was walking out the door one of them said:

"Good luck, Pat, you'll need it."

I then went on to visit a solicitor in a UK based legal firm. He checked the Supply Agreement and pointed out that six months written notice was required for termination of the Agreement by either party. He agreed that our customer was in material breach of the Agreement but that technically the Agreement was still in force because neither party had formally terminated it. He advised that I should write to the customer and give them six months' notice of termination. He also pointed out that I should not approach any other potential customer until expiry of the notice period, otherwise the current customer could claim that WA was in breach of the Agreement. It felt galling that we would have to sit on our hands until January 1989 despite being left for dead by someone else, but such is how the legal process operates and I would just have to accept it.

The solicitor tried to lift my spirits by telling me that we had a good case. He gave me a mountain of paperwork to do to help him prepare our claim. This would cover every detail of our relationship with the customer from the first purchase order, invoices, returned product, damaged product, WIP, stock, etc., in effect anything that was done for or on behalf of the customer. This task would have the added benefit of keeping me busy. The solicitor knew about our financial position and our need to conserve cash, so he said that he would talk to the accounts people and ask them to be flexible with us. I left there in buoyant mood and a growing conviction that I could save WA. I sent the Letter of Termination to the customer and the solicitor sent them notice of our intent to take legal action against them for a

"The Runner"

material breach of contract. We received no immediate response from them.

I went home and immediately started calling all of our other creditors and told them of our dire situation, but that we had initiated legal proceedings against the customer. I also explained that Plessey was willing to give us 12 months to get WA back on its feet. That was not strictly true because I didn't have formal confirmation from Plessey to that effect. On the other hand, I didn't have rejection of it either. I also told them that our technology was highly regarded and that we would have little difficulty in securing new customers.

Amazingly, none of our creditors took action against us. I sent our solicitor the information and the documents he had requested and he just seemed to gobble it up as he requested more information every few days. After a couple of months he seemed to have the bulk of what he needed to prepare a claim. By October 1988 WA had gone four months with no customer and no sales.

I had delayed making as many payments as possible, but some bills couldn't be avoided and cash gradually seeped out of the bank account. One day I arrived at the factory and discovered that the phone was dead. Telecom Eireann had cut off the line for non-payment of a bill, so I had to clear that immediately. That was a salutary lesson to me to pay my phone bills on time in future.

Percy
In December 1988 the outlook for WA was very bleak. The slow drift towards failure seemed inexorable. Several people suggested to me that WA was a lost cause and that I should quit and move on with my life. They meant well, but I felt that I shouldn't quit unless failure was an absolute certainty. Although I didn't want to quit I needed to find some way to keep going. I remembered

"The Runner"

seeing a movie in my childhood that gave me inspiration. The movie was called "Harvey" and it starred James Stewart. Harvey was an imaginary rabbit that James Stewart could see and talk to, and Harvey would give advice to Stewart from time to time. I decided to invent an imaginary character to advise and inspire me, and I called him Percy. Every time I felt mounting pressure to quit I would tell Percy, but Percy wouldn't let me quit. A typical conversation with Percy would go as follows.

Pat: "Percy, I'm not sure I can go on. I'm running out of money. Several people are threatening legal action against me for nonpayment of bills and what they deem to be my reckless trading. I've put up a good fight over many months, but I'm exhausted now and maybe it's time for me to quit."

Percy: "Don't talk to me about quitting. Don't ever talk to me about quitting. Come to me for advice on how to keep going if you wish, but never ever mention that ugly Q word to me again. Stop being a wimp and get on with putting WA back on its feet."

I had several similar conversations with Percy, and he always gave me the lift that kept me going. I am indebted to Percy.

By January 1989 the cash balance was down to just over IR£80,000, but January 1989 was significant for a hugely important reason. That was the month that I could contact potential customers without fear of breaching the Supply Agreement which was now formally terminated.

Reflections on Phase 1 of WA's Life
The first phase of WA's life was now over. It had been a rollercoaster ride. Despite the fact that WA had been mercilessly dumped by the first customer I felt that they had done me a favour by bringing that supply relationship to an end and I was hopeful that I was about to start a new era for WA. Strange as it may seem I had a firm belief that WA could survive and that I would redeem myself. I began to reflect on my business

experience to date and gave some thought to the mistakes I had made, not least of which were:

- Trusting people too much
- Giving a customer exclusivity on our technology
- Using a high volume/low price/low profit margin approach to pricing
- Including delivery in the price

WA – Reboot

In January 1989 I wrote to four of the companies that I had visited in 1985. All responded positively, so I arranged to visit them in February. All of the companies spoke highly of our technology but the first three were talking about a timeframe of at least one year to integrate the technology into their products. WA could hardly survive another few months without a customer, and everything was now riding on the fourth company I visited. The company was MEM, based in Holyhead in Wales.

I met Bob Millican, one of their senior engineers. That's a name of Irish origin, so I wondered if he had Irish connections. He said that he had no direct connections with Ireland, but it transpired that his wife was Irish. Bob and I immediately struck up a good rapport and he explained that MEM was in the process of redesigning their RCD PCB but that due to limited electronic expertise they were struggling with some technical issues. We discussed the project and I told him that I could get five working samples back to him within four weeks free of charge. He was amazed at this and decided to take up my challenge. Bob gave me drawings and samples of their boards and I caught the ferry back to Dublin that evening and dashed back to Ballinasloe to start work on the MEM project. I designed a replacement PCB within a week. I dashed down to Shannon to meet a company that offered a PCB prototyping service. I agreed to pay them cash for six prototypes which I could collect four days later. On the fourth day I again dashed down to Shannon. As I came around the corner of a road

"The Runner"

near Ennis I was taken aback to see a Garda (Irish policeman) standing in the middle of the road about 100 yards ahead. As he raised his hand for me to stop, I noticed a speed limit sign that said 55MPH. I was doing just over 60 MPH. I slowed down gradually so as not to be too obvious about it. When I stopped and wound down the window the Garda came over and said:

"This is a 55MPH stretch and you were doing 63MPH."

I was certainly doing something like that, but this was 1989 and he had no speed detection equipment and yet he gave me a very precise figure. I glanced over at the Garda car by the side of the road and I could see another Garda reading a newspaper, so he didn't seem to have any speed measuring equipment either. In that moment I thought – 'He's bluffing.' I was convinced that there was no way for him to produce such an exact figure for my speed and then my survival instinct kicked in as I replied:

"Actually Garda, I knew you were here. The cars coming towards me were flashing their lights to warn me, and I made sure I was below the 55 MPH limit as I came around that bend."

He looked at me, and looked up at the bend, and by now there were several cars forming an orderly line behind me. He checked my Tax and Insurance discs and told me to be on my way. I continued my trip to Shannon in a more sedate manner. I collected the boards and resisted the urge to break any speed limits on the way home. (A couple of years later I was caught speeding by a Garda with a handheld speed detector, and this time justice was duly served.)

I assembled the electronic circuitry on to the PCBs and tested them to ensure that they met the MEM performance requirements. They worked perfectly so I arranged to travel back to MEM with the samples. It was almost four weeks to the date of my previous visit and Bob was very impressed. Bob's engineers

"The Runner"

said that the samples would have to go through exhaustive testing to ensure compliance with relevant RCD product standards and that this would take six to eight weeks. It was late March 1989, and they said that if all went well we might get a purchase order in May or June. We had just £10,000 left in the bank and I wondered if I could hold out long enough to get MEM on board as a paying customer.

Bob had told me that they would have a possible requirement for around 10,000 PCBs per year and asked me for a unit price. I remembered that with the first customer WA had used a standard "cost plus" model for setting the price of the PCBs but I had already decided that I would never use that model again. I was determined that in future I would set the price based on my sense of the customer's need or my sense of the value of the WA technology to a customer, and this would provide scope for a higher price than a simple "cost plus" model.

I pitched the price at £5.00 per PCB and waited for a reaction. The Technical Director seemed somewhat surprised but then said:

"Let Purchasing sort out the price. Our job was to get a technical solution and we have done that."

The new business would be worth about IR£60,000 per year, and although that would not sustain WA indefinitely, it was a start. My primary objective now was to look after this customer and not give them any cause to regret using WA as a key supplier. However, I needed more customers and it seemed that that could take some time. The question was – how much more time? None of the other companies that I visited in January had followed up with me and I was seriously worried about our ability to survive. It was awful to think that despite having survived a full year and made some progress on the legal front we would finally run out of cash and have to admit failure.

"The Runner"

It was now June 1989 and we had about IR£6,000 left in the bank. In a last desperate throw of the dice I decided to place an advert in an international magazine in which I offered free samples of the WA ASIC to all respondents. I was amazed to receive over 200 responses requesting the free ICs. There were enquiries from the UK and all over Europe including Greece and Turkey, and even Israel. I supplied the free samples, and I was disappointed when I heard nothing back from anybody.

In late June Bob called me to say that MEM would place a P.O. with WA for 10,000 PCBs to be delivered from early August at the rate of 1000 per month. He then surprised me when he said that they had another RCD and that they would like me to design a PCB for that one. The volume of that RCD was also about 10,000 a year and suddenly I was looking at the prospect of annual sales of about IR£120,000. This was incredible news and I felt as if the sun had finally broken through the dark clouds hanging over us. When the P.O. arrived it stated that the price included insurance and delivery. I was determined that WA would not pay for delivery so I called the Purchasing Manager and insisted that WA would not pay for delivery. He said that the price included delivery, but I was adamant that it did not. The caller went quiet for what seemed like ages and we had a standoff. Eventually he said that he would call me back later. This was a crucial matter for me because I knew from our experience with our first customer that shipping costs could seriously erode profit margins. A customer who does not pay for shipping costs can make all sorts of demands on deliveries, e.g., small amounts, more frequent deliveries, or even insist on the use of air freight when sea freight is an option. A few hours later the Purchasing Manager called me to say that they would cover the cost of insurance and delivery.

A lesson I learned from that standoff was that the party with the greater need will usually back down. The purchasing manager didn't know how desperate I was and if he hadn't called back later I would have had to climb down and agree to his terms. We had a

"The Runner"

fair amount of raw stock of components and production materials left over from the first WA era so we would have to buy relatively few new components to get MEM into initial production. Production commenced in July 1989, 13 months after the fateful call doomed WA to closure, but we were about to rise from the dead. The first batch of about 2,000 PCBs was shipped in August 1989. MEM paid promptly at the end of September. It wasn't a lot of money, but I thought that this would be a good time to show good faith to our creditors, so I used about half of the money to send payments to several of them. I did the same thing a month later after which I started to receive calls from several of our creditors expressing surprise at the arrival of the cheques and wanting to know what was happening. I explained that we had a new customer and that we were back in production and that I intended to pay off our entire debt to them as soon as possible. I was then asked whose components I was using, and I said that we had some old stock and we were using that up steadily, but that I didn't expect them to supply us again because of our setback and that I would have to look for new suppliers. Amazingly, every one of our old suppliers offered to supply us again.

In the third quarter of 1989 I received a call from the head of engineering from a German company called Bender. They had been one of the companies who had responded to the advertisement in the international magazine and received free samples. The caller explained that they had spent several months evaluating the samples and that they were impressed with them and would like me to visit them to discuss a possible business opportunity. I visited them within a couple of weeks, and amazingly they trusted me enough to ask me to design a PCB for them. Again, the sales value would be modest enough, but it added credibility to my belief that WA could survive.

My business model for WA now was to do as little as possible for as much as possible, i.e., seek out low volume business and set

"The Runner"

high pricing and refuse to cover delivery costs and thereby maximise our profit margins. We now had two customers that fitted that model.

In October 1989 I received a phone call from the Irish Export Board in Dublin. They said that a company in Australia had contacted them with a query about RCD technology and they gave me contact details. The company was called HPM. I called them and spoke to their Technical Director, Dennis Galvin. HPM were a major supplier of socket outlets to the Australian market, but they had a relatively small portion of the socket-based RCD business. Dennis explained that the Australian product standard for RCDs was due to be changed in January 1990 and that their current RCD could not meet the new requirements. I was aware of the particular issue and confirmed that our technology could meet the requirements. He said he would arrange to send some of the HPM RCDs to me to evaluate with a view to WA designing a replacement PCB. He stressed that speed was of the essence because the new requirements were due to come into effect on 1 January 1990, barely ten weeks away.

The HPM samples arrived by DHL a few days later and I got to work straight away. I spent a whole weekend working on the design and layout and eventually I had a working prototype. I made three prototype samples and sent them to HPM by courier. A few days later I got a call from Dennis saying that he was very impressed with the prototypes and that they would test and evaluate them urgently. Two weeks later I got another call from Dennis to inform me that the units had passed their tests. HPM were currently selling about 10,000 units per year and he wanted an indication price for the PCB. I remembered my lesson from MEM – get the technical people on board first and they will tell Purchasing to buy the product. I pitched the price at IR£4.00, ex-factory, Ballinasloe and Dennis said that that was fine. He said that HPM would place a PO for 10,000 units to be delivered at the rate of about 850 per month. He asked me not to wait for the PO

"The Runner"

to arrive and to gear up for production immediately and get the first shipment out to them in late November or early December at the latest. I expressed my appreciation, and I had no sooner put the phone down than I realised that we had a big problem. In the time that we had available, there was no way I would be able to get custom packaging to ship the PCBs out to Australia. I racked my brain for a solution, and then I had a brainwave. The modules were small enough to fit into a matchbox. Bryant & May were the largest supplier of matches to the Irish market so I contacted their Dublin office to see if I could persuade them to sell WA empty match boxes. They referred me to their head office in Liverpool. When I phoned the Liverpool office and explained to the salesman what I wanted, he burst out laughing. I then heard him shout out to the other people in his office:

"Hay lads, I have an Irish guy on the line who wants to buy 10,000 match boxes, and guess what, he wants us to leave out the matches."

Another guy shouted back:

"Maybe he's trying to reduce the fire risk."

They had a great laugh at my expense, but I was willing to put up with the slagging as long as I got my match boxes. I explained to him that I wanted to ship small electronic PCBs to Australia and that they fitted into match boxes and would be well protected. Once he realised that I was serious and that I really needed their help he agreed to talk to someone there about the possibility of shipping 10,000 unlabelled empty match boxes to Ireland at our expense.

The match boxes arrived a week or so later, and we were able to make our first shipment of PCBs to HPM in December 1989. I received a call from Dennis shortly after they arrived and he said that the people at HPM were amused at our use of matchboxes but admired such innovative packaging.

By early 1990 we had three customers, and my new value-based pricing system would help to assure us of good profitability. However, we seemed to struggle on all fronts with supplies, production, quality, rejects and batch deliveries. I didn't know it at the time but we were facing into a problem of "Organisational Complexity".

Up to 1988, we had had a single customer with a single product and a limited range of components and suppliers. With the continuous flow of a high volume of the same product on a single production line we could become highly efficient and achieve economies of scale. But we now had three customers with five different products and a wider range of components and materials and a growing range of suppliers. The volumes for each product were relatively low and each product was different and required different setup and production processes. Each product had several different components and fittings and a different test specification to meet the customer's specific requirements. We now needed more people to produce these smaller batches of product, more supervision, and more management which drove up costs and reduced profitability. This was a classic example of "increased complexity" in organisational terms and it kills many small firms because they can't manage such complexity.

Although I was not acquainted at that time with terms like "organisational complexity", I didn't need a fancy name or a degree in management to see the dangers facing us. It was very fortunate that I had abandoned the 'cost-plus' approach to pricing and simply asked for the highest price I thought I could get for each new product because although profitability fell due to the less efficient production runs, we had enough head room to get by in the short term and we just had to learn how to improve efficiency. Over the

"The Runner"

following months we started to improve our manufacturing processes and the WA ship began to stabilise once again.

1990 "WA Lift Off"?

We had shipped product to HPM at the rate of about 1000 units in December, January and February of 1990. I got a call from Dennis in early March and to my pleasant surprise he told me to ship the balance of the 10,000-unit order as soon as possible and said that HPM would place another PO for 20,000 units. He said that the sudden increase in demand arose because HPM were just one of two companies supplying RCDs to the Australian market that were in compliance with the new 1990 regulations. The competitors who hadn't upgraded their products were excluded from the market pending a suitable upgrade of their products.

A key lesson to emerge from that experience was that technology companies should embrace change and not resist it. By embracing change WA had become a significant player in the Australian RCD market.

In March 1990, our solicitor Bob contacted me to say that they had completed the "discovery" process and that he had some news for me.

"Hi, Pat. Are you sitting down?"

I said "Yes". I was expecting some bad news, but he almost knocked me off the chair when he said:

"Pat, we are looking at a claim for around £200,000."

For a moment I felt like I had won the Lotto, and then came the caveat:

"The Runner"

"Pat, the legal process could take another two years because I would expect the opposition to drag this out for as long as possible. We will need to involve a barrister and the legal costs will rise sharply. WA will need to fund that and survive long enough to get us to court, otherwise our claim will collapse."
This was a bittersweet moment, but I preferred to focus on the sweet part. I gave Bob the good news about our newfound customers. He was delighted and wished me continued success in adding to the customer base. In early 1990 we produced our first set of audited account for the period January 1985 to December 1989. They showed an aggregate turnover of about IR£1.75m and an aggregate loss of about IR£32,000. Cash had grown to about IR£27,000, but we had debts of about IR£100,000. We no longer had raw stock from the first WA era, and we were now having to buy new components and materials. These new purchases and payments against our old debts were draining our cash reserves. I knew that we were currently trading profitably and that our debts were historical and giving a misleading impression. Nonetheless, running out of cash would threaten the survival of the company at a time when we were on the road to recovery. We would just have to continue on that road and try to operate as efficiently as possible.

I realised that one of my major weaknesses to date had been my lack of management expertise. I already had management experience, but not a sound understanding of how to manage a business. I knew that my "seat of the pants" style of management would not sustain WA and I needed to address that. I considered going to evening classes but I couldn't find any suitable courses on offer near Ballinasloe. I then came up with the idea of enrolling with the Open University, and in 1990 I signed up with them to do a Diploma in Professional Management. The program was set out in modular form so that students could choose the modules to study as they wished. I started with "Finance & Accountancy for Managers" and progressed to Production Management, Recruiting & Selecting People, followed by Sales & Marketing.

"The Runner"

The courses were excellent, and I started to get a better understanding about Operations and Finance.

WA – A Social Role

Unemployment was still very high in Ireland in 1990 and WA received job applications in the post almost every week, but I needed to contain costs and avoid taking on too many employees. However, one day I received a job application from a girl named Tammy. It appeared from her CV that she had left school at 15 and she was now 16 years old and looking for a job. I would not normally interview someone who had given up school early, but something about her covering letter intrigued me and persuaded me to interview her. I asked her the obvious question about not finishing school. She told me that her family were Jehovah's Witnesses and that her parents insisted that she leave school at 15 so that she could spend a year working for the Church. This involved going door to door trying to recruit people to the Church and handing out leaflets, etc. Her year of service was completed and she was now in need of money and desperate for a job.

During the interview I recalled my own experience of being pushed into a hut at age 16 and asking for a job. I decided to take her on as a Production Operative and it turned out to be one of the best decisions I made around that time because she proved to be a superb employee. Two years later I promoted her to Production Supervisor. She got married when she was 20 and emigrated to Canada. She came to see me a few years later when she came back to Ireland for a family visit.

A few weeks after recruiting Tammy I got a call from Pat McGovern who was well known in Ballinasloe for his work in the local musical society. Pat asked if he could call in to see me about something and I met him that evening when the

"The Runner"

employees had left the factory. Pat said that a neighbour of his was very distraught and had asked him to approach me about the possibility of giving her daughter a job. It transpired that the 17-year-old daughter was planning to go to England because she couldn't get a job in Ireland, and this was the mothers youngest child. I told Pat that we had no vacancies but he pleaded with me to at least interview the girl and then decide whether to give her a job or not. Pat was very persuasive, so I reluctantly agreed.

A date and time was set for the interview and the mother arrived with her very shy timid daughter. I asked the girl to follow me into my small office and I was shocked when the mother came in too. I explained to the mother that I needed to speak to her daughter alone and that she should wait outside. The mother was reluctant to leave so I said that if this girl was to get a job anywhere she would need to undergo an interview on her own and get the job on her own merits and not because of her mother's influence.

I interviewed the girl and she told me that her siblings had gone to England and whilst she wanted to stay in Ireland she felt she had no option but to follow suit. I decided to take her on, and she too turned out to be an excellent employee. A few years later she got married and quit her job to have a family.

In 1995 I held a tenth-year anniversary dinner for the employees and customers and suppliers who had helped WA to reach that milestone. I allowed each employee to bring a guest and we had over 100 people at the dinner which was held in Hayden's Hotel in Ballinasloe.

At the dinner I gave a speech about WA's journey to date. I mentioned that WA had grown to serve a social role in Ballinasloe through its employment, etc. and I told the story about that girl by way of an example. After the speech I started to mingle amongst the guests and I was shocked when one of the employees introduced me to her friend. It was the "17-year-old

"The Runner"

girl", but she was now married and the proud mother of two children and they lived just outside Ballinasloe. She laughed as she reminded me of the interview that I almost had with her mother.

Those two recruitments opened my eyes to the role that businesses, large and small, play in the social fabric of our towns. I continued with my studies with the Open University throughout 1990 and 1991 and I was awarded a Diploma in Professional Management in 1991. That education enabled me to think more like a manager and I began to reflect on how WA should be managed going forward. I realised that I had been trying to do too much myself, largely to save costs. However, I needed to act more like a company manager and not continue in the roles of design engineer, production manager, quality manager and supply chain manager, etc. so I started recruiting people to perform those tasks. Fortunately, EI provided grants against the first year's salaries for these new recruits.

Small, But No Pushover
WA had signed a Supply Agreement with a company who wanted us to supply one of their subsidiary companies with our technology. The Supply Agreement was fair and balanced and very much in line with similar agreements that we had with other customers. However, the purchasing manager in the subsidiary company wanted to have his own Supply Agreement specifically suited to the subsidiary company. The proposed alternative Agreement set out very onerous terms that were totally unacceptable to WA. The purchasing manager insisted that WA sign the new Agreement, but I refused. He started to send abusive messages and made threats about not paying our invoices and I needed to find a way to defuse the situation, so I decided to send him a letter as follows.

"The Runner"

Dear Jim,

As you know, WA has signed a Supply Agreement with your parent company and both parties to that Agreement are quite happy with it. Nonetheless you keep insisting that WA must adopt your proposed Supply Agreement and you have even threatened us with non-payment of invoices. As far as we are concerned, your Agreement does not exist. I have tried to explain this to you several times but you still persist with your demands for us to operate to a non-existent Supply Agreement.

Your behaviour reminds me of the story of a lady who went into a fishmonger shop to buy cod, and that conversation went along the following lines.

Lady: "Hi, I would like a pound of cod."
Shop owner: "I'm sorry madam but we have run out of cod. Can I offer you something else?"
Lady: "No, I want cod. This is a fish shop. You must have cod. I want cod."
Shop owner: "I'm so sorry madam but we have no cod."
Lady: "Nonsense. You always have cod. I want my cod and I'm not leaving here until I get it."
Shop owner: I'm truly sorry madam but I can assure you that we do not have any cod"
Lady: "I don't believe you. You must have cod."
Shop owner in desperation: "Madam, would you mind doing me a favour and spelling the word cod."
Lady: "What nonsense is that? I just want my cod."
Shop owner: "Please madam, just humour me and spell the word cod. Please."
Lady: "OK, C-O-D. Now can I have my cod?"
Shop owner: "Now madam, I have just one more small request. Would you mind spelling the word cod without the letter F."
Lady: "You stupid man, there is no F in COD."
Shop owner. "Precisely madam. That's what I've been trying to tell you. Good day madam."

"The Runner"

So do me a favour, Jim, and spell the word AGREEMENT without the letter F.

I await your reply.

Pat Ward - Managing Director

A few weeks later we were informed that Jim was no longer employed by the subsidiary company.

The Irish Management Institute
In August 1991 I saw an advertisement from the Irish Management Institute (IMI) promoting one of its management courses, a Master of Science (MSc) degree in Management Practice. I was immediately attracted to the idea of doing such a course for two reasons.

1. I had learned a lot about basic management from my two-year Diploma program with the Open University, and I now had a hunger to learn about strategic management, which the MSc course offered.

2. Given that this was a Master of Science degree and not a Master of Business Administration degree, I realised that it would involve the practical application of management theory and techniques to a business, and that appealed to me in terms of the possible application of this program to WA.

Being the eternal optimist, I applied to the IMI and I was greatly surprised to be accepted on to the program which started in September 1991.

On the first morning of the course, 12 successful applicants sat in a classroom, ten men and two women. The course director

"The Runner"

welcomed us and set out the objectives of the two-year course and wished us well. He then asked each of us to introduce ourselves and to state what business we were in.

The first person was a senior manager in Aer Lingus and he explained how Aer Lingus transported people and goods around Europe and between North America and Ireland. I was very impressed with his introduction.

The next candidate said that he was a director with Coilte, the Irish Forestry Agency, and explained that they grew and harvested trees for the wood industry.

The next candidate was a senior manager with Bord Na Mona, the Irish government agency dealing with extraction of turf from Irish bogs for use as fuel in homes and power stations.

I was beginning to feel a bit out of my depth amongst these industrial giants given that I ran a micro company, and our annual turnover would not even cover the canteen bill of any of the companies mentioned so far. I began to think about how I would introduce myself and WA. As I reflected on the previous introductions I felt that something was missing from their answers. I reminded myself of the question:

What business are you in?

I then realised that not one of the previous candidates had provided the precise answer to that question, and suddenly it was my turn to introduce myself and answer the question.

"Hi, my name is Pat Ward. My company is called Western Automation Research & Development.

We are in the business of profitably meeting the needs of our customers.

"The Runner"

We do that by providing RCD technology to our customers. They integrate our technology into their products and sell those products on to their customers."

The director smiled at my answer and moved on to the next candidate who introduced himself as the manager of a company that was the main importer and distributor of the USA Southern Comfort drink in Ireland.

When the introductions were completed the director said, "Thank you all for the introductions. The question I asked was:

What business are you in?

Only one of you gave a satisfactory answer. Congratulations Pat Ward on your answer. You said that you were in the business of profitably meeting the needs of your customers. You then explained how you do that.

You all need to realise that every for-profit organisation is first and foremost in the business of making money, i.e., generating profits, and how you do that is another matter. Most of you told me what you did in terms of products or services but you didn't mention making money. Any commercial business that cannot generate profits will not be able to continue to provide products or a service to customers, so your focus must on generating profits."

Suddenly I didn't feel so much out of my depth amongst these industrial giants. That message became embedded in my brain from that day onwards. WA was in the business of making money. We did that by selling RCD technology, but in time we might do it be selling something else, and therein lies a clue to long term business success. All successful businesses adapt. They don't continue indefinitely doing the same old thing because sooner or later that business model will become obsolete or be bettered by a competitor.

"The Runner"

WA is in the business of profitably meeting the needs of its customers.

It seemed that to date WA had been meeting the needs of customers, but not always doing so profitably.

I spent an average of two days per month attending classes at the IMI, with the occasional additional weekend thrown in for workshops, etc., all of this whilst also managing WA. Over the first year or so of the MSc I did a lot of business research and learned a lot about business strategy, management principles and business models. Many of the models or principles seemed to be designed with large companies in mind and not targeted at small businesses. Every company wants to have a competitive advantage but I ran a micro company and I struggled to see how such a small company could find, let alone exploit, a competitive advantage. However, a competitive advantage would come from an unexpected source.

International Standards Bodies
In September 1991 I received a call from Bob Millican asking me to arrange to come to Birmingham to meet him and two of his colleagues on a Saturday!! I asked him why he wanted to meet on a Saturday and he replied that it would be a private meeting at a local hotel at 2pm. I agreed to get a flight to Birmingham and meet with them. However, I was seriously unhappy because that was the date of the first match of the Rugby World Cup Competition to be played between England and Australia. I was very keen to watch that match, but it now looked like I would have to miss it.

I arrived at the hotel in plenty of time for the 2.00pm meeting and Bob introduced me to his two colleagues, Arnold Horton from Wylex, and John Rickwood from Crabtree, two companies that I

"The Runner"

had visited when trying to get WA started. Bob explained that the purpose of the meeting was to discuss a document that had been presented to Cenelec setting out new requirements for RCDs. Cenelec is the body responsible for setting up product standard requirements for electrical products supplied to European markets. To date, the only requirement for RCDs was to comply with a British Standard, but Bob explained that because of EU membership all RCDs would have to comply with the requirements of Cenelec from 1992 onwards, and they were concerned that their current RCDs would not meet the requirements and thus be excluded from the UK as well as European markets.

This had echoes of HPM about it and I assumed that Cenelec had simply adopted similar requirements, so I was confident that our RCD technology would comply with the new requirements. However, a quick reading of the proposals in the Cenelec document revealed that the new technical requirements were likely to prove to be a big challenge to WA and its customers. Bob and his colleagues conveyed a palpable sense of tension as I scanned the document over and over again. Finally Bob couldn't wait any longer and said:

"Well, what do you think?"

I replied, "I think we should go into the bar and watch the England – Australia match."

Bob nearly had a heart attack, but John and Arnold thought that was a great idea and we trundled off to the bar to watch the match. When the match ended Bob blurted:

"Can we discuss the document now?"

I explained that the document seemed to be contrived and intended to drive competitors out of the market. In effect, it was anti-competition and had little to do with standardisation. The question was how to deal with it. If the proposals were adopted, WA and its customers would be shut out of the market with no quick way of re-entering it. John informed me that a meeting to discuss the proposals in the document had been arranged for the following month in Brussels and he wanted me to come along. He explained that I would need to inform the National Standards Authority of Ireland (NSAI) and ask for permission to represent Ireland at the meeting.

A whole new world of Standardisation was about to open up for me, and it would have a massive impact on WA over the coming years. The NSAI enrolled me into Cenelec and the IEC (the International Electrical Commission) and gave me approval to represent Ireland at the Brussels meeting. My three newfound amigos and I agreed that we would reject the document proposals on the grounds of anti-competitive practice and refuse to discuss the technical proposals. I felt that most of the member countries present would have no desire to be associated with what might be perceived as anti-competitive practice, and the document was duly withdrawn.

This was the first time that I had attended an international meeting dealing with Standardisation of RCD products, and it demonstrated to me the advantages to be gained by participating in the work of such bodies. By attending that meeting in Brussels we had averted a serious threat to WA's business, but I knew that such threats would recur. Through participation in Standards bodies a company can get an insight into the drafting of national or international product standards and advance notice of likely future requirements. In effect, those bodies set out the future direction of the industry and companies that fail to participate are at a disadvantage vis-à-vis those that do participate. Up to that meeting in Brussels, WA had been producing RCD designs based on current requirements with no way of knowing what would be required in the future. WA would have been a reactive participant in the industry, but through participation in Standardisation bodies WA could become a proactive participant and stay ahead of non-participating competitors. That chance meeting in Birmingham was about to transform WA.

Immediately following from the Brussels meeting I directed that all product design work in WA be based on future proposals or requirements and no longer on current requirements.

WA products would be future proofed, and WA and its customers would reap the benefits. This provided WA with a competitive advantage over companies that did not participate in the work of such bodies. IEC and CENELEC meetings were typically attended by delegates from some 20 to 30 countries and this provided WA with forums in which to promote WA and to enable WA to seek out potential customers. Being able to participate in discussions on complex topics such as product design, product reliability, electromagnetic compatibility etc. enabled me to project the notion that WA had expertise in these fields. Many of the participating delegates came from companies who needed such expertise, and WA was willing and able to provide it. It would not be an overstatement to say that IEC and Cenelec enabled WA to achieve global recognition and branding in a way that no amount of advertising could have achieved.

Over the following 25 years, I would travel to more than thirty counties to attend an average of two IEC or Cenelec meetings per year, and my work in those bodies would expand from RCDs and electric shock protection to arc fault protection and on to protection of Electric Vehicles (EVs) during charging. Participation in International Standards bodies had enabled me to scan the world for business opportunities, to anticipate new or emerging needs, and to prepare to meet those needs. Over time, customers would develop a dependency on WA to act as its eyes and ears when it came to meeting current regulations, anticipating new regulations, and ensuring ongoing and seamless compliance with the new regulations.

"The Runner"

The IEC meetings were hosted by different countries from around the world and the host country would designate a city to hold the event. I was pleasantly surprised when South Africa chose Durban as the city for a conference. I had my prior memories of Durban, but this time I was older and wiser, and I didn't need anyone to tell me to avoid the Cane wine and the local women.
WA acquired two new customers in late 1991, Ashley & Rock and Legrand. These were both small accounts, but very welcome. It seemed that I was now building a solid foundation for growth. However, the MEM business also started to increase that year and we were running into capacity problems in our small premises so I started searching around for a larger premises but there was no suitable building available in Ballinasloe. I spotted an area of industrial zoned land for sale on the other side of town. It was about 4 acres and was on the market for IR£40,000, much too expensive for WA. The local auctioneer told me that the land was owned by Telecom Eireann (yes, the same company that had disconnected my phone in 1988). The land had been on the market for three years with no offers to buy it because it was considered overpriced. I was told by the auctioneer that TE had paid an inflated price for the land and never went ahead with plans for its use, and they were now stuck with an overpriced asset. I sent a letter to the TE company headquarters in Dublin expressing my interest in buying the land and asking for an appointment to discuss it with someone. To my surprise I was invited to a meeting at the head office in Dublin.

In those pre-motorway days, it took at least three hours to drive from Ballinasloe to Dublin. At times on that drive I pondered at the futility of the trip, but convinced myself that I would have no chance of success if I didn't try. Better to try and fail than fail to try.

I parked my car at a nearby car park and made my way to their headquarters which turned out to be a massive multi story building. I went up an elevator to the top floor and I was asked to

"The Runner"

wait in a reception area. Finally, I was taken into a room where there were six people from the property department. I explained that I had started a small electronics company in Ballinasloe and that we had outgrown our current premises and that I wished to buy an acre of land so that I could build a small factory unit. They smiled and someone said that they had no intention of selling the land piecemeal. I explained that I couldn't afford the asking price of IR£40,000. I was asked to wait outside. A short time later a man came out of the room and explained that TE wanted to sell the land in one lot, and he asked me what I could afford for the lot. I said that I could possibly pay IR£20,000 with a bank loan. I had no reason to believe that the bank would lend me the money, but I had to persuade TE to sell before I would need to jump the loan hurdle. The man went back into the room and I sat outside and agonised over what they might decide. He came out a few minutes later and said that they had agreed to accept my offer of IR£20,000. I was both shocked and delighted. He then told me that he had been born and raised in Aughrim village, just outside Ballinasloe and that he had gone to school in Ballinasloe. He managed to persuade his colleagues to put the land to good use by supporting a Ballinasloe based Irish start-up technology company. I expressed my gratitude to them all and headed back to Ballinasloe.

I was euphoric at my success, and then realised that they weren't aware that I had been a delinquent customer whose phone had been disconnected due to late payment. Thank God for large companies with departments that do not speak to each other. I contacted ICC Bank, (The Industrial Credit Corporation), a small state-run bank that was set up to help Irish businesses. I told them about our terrible set-back in 1988 and explained that we were now growing rapidly, and WA needed to secure a loan to buy the land. They backed me and gave me the loan.

"The Runner"

A local man named Val Martin designed an 8,000 square foot building and he duly produced the drawings and submitted them on our behalf for planning permission. That was quickly granted, and the new factory was completed and opened in January 1992. We had gone from a 1000 square foot premises to an 8000 square foot factory and the place sounded like an echo chamber initially, but we grew into it over time.

I asked Val to send me an invoice for his work but as the weeks went by no invoice arrived. I pestered him for an invoice, and he finally sent one in for £400!! I called him and asked him if that was to be a part payment, but he said it was the full amount. I said it was too low and asked him to increase it, but he replied that he

was pleased to an Irish technology company in Ballinasloe and he wished me well.

Sadly, Val Martin passed away in 2022.

We were better able to organise the production process in the new premises, and we even set up a dedicated area for product design, our first R & D centre. Things were looking good, and I continued my studies with the IMI.

I was interested in how best to manage growth and I did a lot of research into this area which revealed that many companies went out of business while growing. Further research indicated that a key cause of failure during the growth phase was a failure to plan and prepare for growth and a failure to anticipate the stresses and strains that could overstretch and overwhelm a growing company. In effect, chasing sales instead of chasing profits proved to be fatal to many growing businesses.

I had to submit my thesis by September 1993, and I came up with the title:

"The Runner"

Sales – Not The Elixir Of Growth For The Small Firm

Growth is like medication. A little can do you good but too much can kill you. Too many sales without the structure and financial strength to support it is a recipe for disaster, and I would remind myself of that constantly over the next 30 years.

By the end of the MSc program in 1993, I had formulated the view that I needed to strengthen WA in order to increase its chances of survival and to support growth. This would not be done by pursuing increased sales (although that is an important requirement in the longer term), but instead by trying to prioritise an increase in profitability so as to strengthen WA and enable it to acquire more resources to facilitate growth.
I felt that I was ready to put this theory to the test for WA.

I was awarded my MSc in September 1993, and I had the added surprise of being presented with the Sir Charles Harvey Award for being the best student in our cohort.

(Sir Charles Harvey was a former chairman of Guinness Brewery Company)

WA was the smallest company participating on that program, but I feel that WA got far more out of it than any of the other participants.

In 1994 I was invited by the Irish Management Institute (IMI) to give talks to budding entrepreneurs who were on one of the IMI's business start-up training programs. The IMI wanted me to tell the WA story in the hope that it would inspire the participants, and I think it did to some extent. At one of the workshops, I talked about the pressures on me to quit WA after the setback in 1988. I told the class about Percy and the way he helped me to keep going.

"The Runner"

One of the class asked me if Percy had a second name, and I said, "Yes, he does."

I then wrote his full name on the board:

PERCY VERANCE = P E R S E V E R A N C E

Percy never quits.

Putting Theory into Practice

As I headed into 1994 I felt it was time to try to put some of the management theory into practice. I felt that WA had been on a continuous roller coaster ride since 1985 and it was time to replace the recurring turbulence with order and stability.

We took on more customers in 1994 and 1995. This placed ever increasing demands on my time with more travel to customers or visits from customers, etc. All of that was coupled with travel to IEC and Cenelec meetings around the world, and as I look back on that period I am amazed at how I coped.

Around that time I was travelling to meetings in Paris and Brussels about two or three times a year so I decided to try to learn some French. I just wanted to reach a level that would make it easier to get around, or order a meal in a restaurant if the staff didn't speak English. Although far from fluent, I tried using my French whenever I got a chance. On one occasion I was attending an IEC meeting in Paris and a group of about 12 delegates decided to go to a local restaurant for an evening dinner. The group comprised of three French guys, one German, two Italians. an American, some Brits and me. We were seated at a long table and as soon as the waiter arrived I began to wonder if I should try ordering my starter in French. The waiter made his way around the table taking the orders and finally arrived at me.

"The Runner"

"Je voudrais... "

Suddenly there were gasps of surprise followed by derision at my attempt to speak French, but the waiter was very supportive and said:

"Monsieur, ignore these stupid people. I will assist you with placing your order in French."

I went on to order my starter and my main course. The wine started to flow, and the waiter would check in on me every now and again to ask me how was the food and the wine and I would reply in French. I discovered that the more wine I drank the more my confidence grew and the more fluent I seemed to be getting in French. Finally, the waiter arrived to take our dessert order, and without looking at the menu I had already decided what I wanted.

Waiter: "Monsieur?
Pat: "Je voudrais des pommes de terre et de la glace, s'il vous plait."
The French speakers at the table erupted in laughter and the waiter said:
"Monsieur, do you know what you have just ordered?"
I replied: "Yes, I ordered apple pie and ice cream."
Waiter: "I'm sorry monsieur but you ordered potatoes and ice cream.

Arghhhh. The wine, the wine. That was my undoing.
The English speakers now joined in the laughter and they would always recommend that I have potatoes with ice cream for my dessert whenever we ate out again.

There was a growing perception in Enterprise Ireland that WA was a growing success, and this manifested itself in the form of awards.

"The Runner"

In 1992 WA won a business award from Wang/IDA, and in 1996 WA won a business award from Ulster bank. We didn't enter any competitions and we didn't have an account with Ulster Bank, but someone somewhere was nominating WA for awards. I wish I could win golf competitions without entering them!!

In June 1992 I received a call from a man named Roger who had recently been appointed Managing Director of our first customer company, asking me to meet with him in Dublin. We met a week or so later and he said that the directors wanted to know if I would be agreeable to an out of court settlement of our claim. Our solicitor had warned me that whilst we had a good case, things could sometimes go awry in court on a technicality or a point of law, and a legal settlement could be up to two years away. I reminded Roger that our claim was for £200,000 but said that I would settle for £100,000 if it was paid promptly. He asked if there was any scope for movement on that and I said:

"Certainly, you can always increase it."

He smiled and said he would report back to the directors. A week later I was invited by a director to meet with him in England.
He asked me if I played golf and I said, "Yes, rather badly."
He suggested that we have a round of golf and asked me to bring my golf shoes. He picked me up at Luton airport and took me to a fancy golf resort. He had a spare set of golf clubs all ready for me, and when we stood on the first tee I rather cheekily suggested that we play a match for £1.00. We made our way around the golf course and chatted about this and that, and we finally arrived at the 17th hole. I had the honour and stepped on to the tee-box. Just as I was about to hit my drive he said:

"Pat, we have almost finished the round of golf. When are we going to discuss the big problem."

"The Runner"

I replied, "I'm one up in the match and if I win this hole you will have to pay me £1.00. That's my only concern just now."

He laughed at me and I went on to win the match and he paid me £1.00. We went into the clubhouse for some lunch and then we got around to discussing the "big problem". He offered me £75,000 in settlement of our dispute and I told him I wouldn't budge from £100,000. I was surprised when he quickly agreed and said that I would receive the payment once the legal issues were resolved. I have won a few fivers in golf over the years, but I have never come away from a golf match winning £100,001!!

Two weeks later we received a payment for £100,000. Our outstanding legal fees came to £40,000, leaving WA with £60,000. I had to smile to myself when I recalled the conversation with that customer back in 1988, when all I asked for a was payment of outstanding invoices and immediate termination of the Supply Agreement. My solicitor reckoned that the opposition had paid about £200,000 in legal fees!!

The new funds enabled me to recruit more engineers and increase our R & D capabilities with a view to fuelling growth. By the end of 1993 sales to MEM had grown substantially and they were now our biggest customer and I felt totally secure with them and saw little or no risk of losing them. However, in 1994 MEM informed me that they had developed their own RCD technology to replace the WA technology and the sudden drop in sales would have a big impact on sales and profits.

We tend to think of competitors as other companies that supply similar technology but I soon realised that the engineers in a customer company were also potential competitors and that they could replace us more easily than direct competitors. The loss of MEM resulted in a substantial reduction in sales in 1995. Fortunately WA was acquiring new customers at a rate

"The Runner"

sufficient to offset the loss of MEM, and within a year or so we were back on a growth trend.

One of our new customers was an Indian company based in New Delhi. I had been to Delhi several times previously so I was quite relaxed about making this trip. On arrival in Delhi I had to get a taxi to my hotel. My flight arrived at about 11.00am and it was about midday when I got into the taxi. I gave the taxi driver the name of my hotel and we started on our journey of about 40 minutes. After about 10 minutes, the taxi driver said,
"Sir, it's very hot. Would you like me to put on the
air conditioning?"

I replied: "Yes please."

Driver: "There will be a 10% surcharge on the fare for use of the air conditioning sir. Is that OK?"

Me: "In that case don't bother with the air conditioning."

Driver: "But sir, it's very hot and you won't be able to tolerate the heat."

Me: "Well I'm not going to pay for air conditioning."

Driver: "OK sir, but you will soon find it too hot."

Sure enough the taxi began to heat up, so I took off my jacket and tie. A short while later I opened both windows in the back of the taxi. However, the taxi moved slowly through Delhi's crowded streets and there wasn't much of a breeze through the open windows.

Driver: "Sir, you are clearly too hot and you really should allow me to put on the air conditioning."

Me: "I'm not stopping you from putting on the air conditioning. I'm just refusing to pay for it."

"The Runner"

After about 20 minutes or so I knew that we had passed the halfway mark and I had no doubt that I could brazen out this extortionate taxi driver. He pleaded with me one more time, but I was not going to be exploited and his plea fell on deaf ears. Finally, we arrived at the hotel and I gave the driver the fare on the meter and no tip.

The driver asked me where I came from and I said "England"!! Well I certainly wasn't going to besmirch the good name of Ireland.
I arrived at the hotel soaking wet, but I felt quite pleased that I had won the battle of wills with that driver. I went to my room and had a nice shower and freshened up.

A few days later I got a taxi from Delhi back to the airport. Shortly after the trip started the driver asked me if I would like him to turn on the air conditioning.

I replied: "Yes please".
He replied: "Certainly, sir" and he turned on the air conditioning.

I gave him a nice tip when we arrived at the airport.

An Illusion of Success
Although the sales and profits figures looked impressive I was aware that they were giving a misleading impression of WA performance, as a look at the Operating Profit would verify.

"The Runner"

Chart 1 – Sales

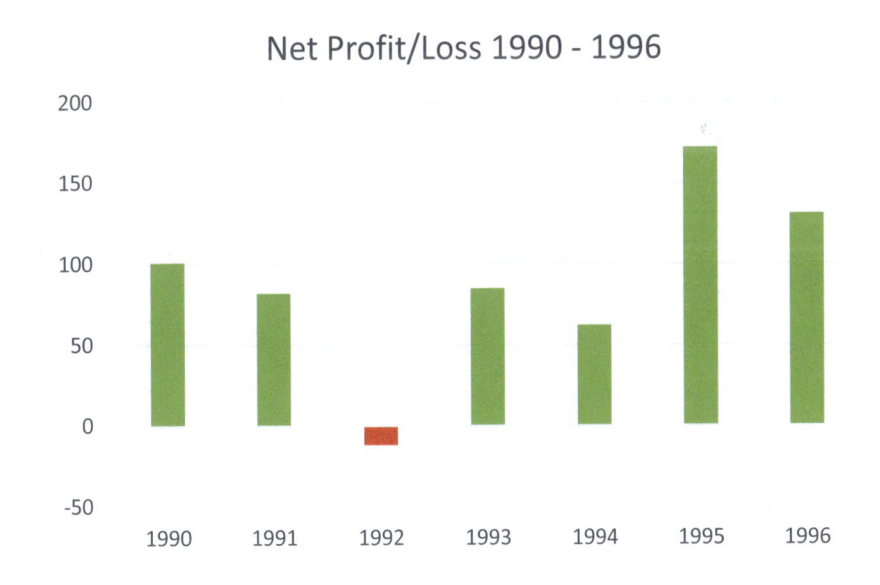

Chart 2 – Net Profit/Loss

"The Runner"

These charts certainly gave the impression of a company on an upward trend, but I reminded myself of that old saying:
Sales = Vanity, Profits = Sanity.

In assessing the profitability of a company, it is normal practice to look at Net profit and to accept that as an indicator of performance. However, the sanity check requires us to take a closer look at what we mean by the term "profits". Net profits can include unearned income in the form of grants or one-off payments or even tax credits that will not recur. By looking at Operating Profits we see only the income generated from trading without the distorting effect of one-off payments, as shown by Chart 3.

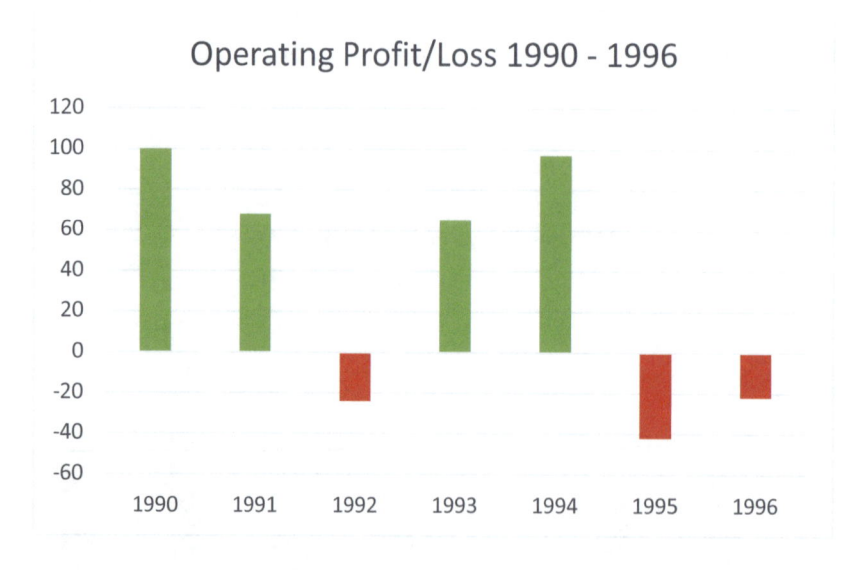

Operating Profit/Loss 1990 - 1996

Chart 3 – Operating Profit/Loss

Chart 3 shows that WA had failed to make an operating profit in three of the latest five years.

If allowed to continue, the erosion in Operating Profits would take WA on a path towards failure. I needed to take effective remedial action.

"The Runner"

I was totally engrossed in WA when I received a call in 1996 that shocked me. Pearl's husband Leo worked as a supervisor in the sewage department of Dublin Corporation. That morning Leo went to inspect a section of the sewage works. After opening a hatch he had to descend a ladder to carry out the inspection, but for some reason he wasn't wearing a protective mask and as he made his descent he was overcome by fumes and fell into the water and drowned.

Pearl adored Leo and he was very good to me. This was my first experience of grief which engulfed me and stifled me and left me struggling to come to terms with how suddenly and unexpectedly a life can end.

I dashed to Dublin to be with Pearl. Val flew over from England and we met up and went to Pearl's house. The house was full of sympathisers, but I was surprised at the scene when Pearl brought the two of us into the living room. Most of the people there were standing or sitting alongside the walls of the room, as if clinging to them. There was one elderly woman sitting in a chair all alone in the middle of the room. I didn't know the woman, but for some strange reason Pearl made a special effort to introduce me to her.

The woman was sitting with a whiskey glass in her hand and as Pearl started to introduce me the woman held out her glass for a refill. Pearl reached for a whiskey bottle and topped up the glass. In her desire to impress the woman Pearl started singing my praises and I found that highly embarrassing, but as I tried to stop Pearl she insisted on blurting out that I had my own business and that I represented Ireland on international committees, etc. It was obvious that this woman had no interest in what Pearl was saying about me and as I tried to draw Pearl away from her she reached out again with her glass for another top-up and Pearl duly obliged. It became obvious that the other people in the room were hugging the walls in order to stay a safe distance from the woman who was firmly intent on getting drunk. Finally, I pulled Pearl

"The Runner"

away and reminded her that we were there to mourn Leo and not to sing my praises.

Pearl needed some groceries so Val and I offered to go to a local shop to collect them for her. About 30 minutes later we returned with the goods and we then went back into the room to have a chat with some relatives and friends. As I was walking across the room the drunken woman shouted at me:

"You, you, you are nothing. You with your notions of attending international conferences. You are nothing but crap, just like your sister. Do you hear me – crap."

I was shocked at the outburst, but also angry at the insult about Pearl. There are times in life when something happens and you want to react, but how do you react to an insulting drunken woman? I have often found that after an event like that I later find the words I wish I had said at the time, but the opportunity to utter them had passed. However, I had a moment of inspiration on this occasion, and as I stood there facing that woman I looked her in the eye and said:

"I'm not crap. The Craps live across the road. There's Momma Crap, Papa Crap and their daughter Alotta Crap, and I believe they're related to you."

The room erupted in laughter and she was shocked at the response, but too drunk to understand what people were laughing at. I was happy to leave her in her drunken stupor.

The funeral was a terribly sad affair and I found myself grieving for days afterwards. Immersing myself back into WA helped me to assuage my grief.

I began to feel seriously overstretched and that I simply didn't have the ability to perform a proper management role in WA.

"The Runner"

I then came up with an idea to invite two people to join me on what I named the CRB – a Company Review Board. This was not a formal or a legal entity, but simply an advisory body. I invited two people with a wealth of business experience to join my CRB. Fortunately for me Eamon Balfe and Dick Blake agreed to sign up.

I explained that in broad terms, I wanted to set WA on a growth path and that I hoped to use their experience and expertise to help me to achieve that, and I set down just two key requirements for the CRB.

1   The meetings must be held off site, e.g., in a hotel.
2   I would not chair the meetings.

The reason that I wanted the meetings off site was because my experience to date had been that when meetings were held at the factory premises there would always be distractions or disruptions that would interrupt the flow of the meetings. And the reason I did not want to chair the meetings was because I wanted to be challenged in my thinking about WA.

Eamon agreed to be the chairman, and I left it to Eamon and Dick to come up with an agenda for the first CRB meeting which was held at the Shamrock Lodge Hotel in Athlone in early 1997. They set me the following tasks.

1. P W. to give an overview of the factors which led to the present business plan and development programme.
2. Operation of the CRB to be as follows.
   Purpose: To receive, consider and comment on reports from Management on the operation and plans of the Company.
   To provide advice and assistance to Management on the operation and development of the Company.
   Meetings scheduled to be two monthly in principle but decided on a case-by-case basis.

"The Runner"

Meetings to be in 3rd or 4th week of the month when accounts for the preceding period would be available.
One meeting each year to focus on updating medium term business plan and one meeting each year to focus on budget for the following year.
All meetings to consider key figures from the Management Accounts.

Transformational
It can be immediately seen that this methodical approach to reviewing WA performance and setting out initial objectives would be transformational if implemented fully and honestly, and it certainly fitted in extremely well with the concept of transitioning WA from an entrepreneurial to a professionally managed business. I came away from that first meeting exhausted but elated. I felt that if I could follow up on the tasks set by the CRB, then over time WA would be on its way to becoming a professionally managed business.

For the first time since starting WA, I found myself accountable. Instead of selectively doing whatever I wanted when I wanted and how I wanted, I now found that I had to do what the CRB deemed most important. The CRB imposed a discipline on me that required me to make the time to respond to CRB requests and to prepare my reports by set deadlines. I had to respect my CRB colleagues and the effort they were putting into their roles, and without that overarching pressure I would almost certainly have drifted back to my old habits of making myself too busy doing other less important things instead of carrying out key management functions. Instead of trying to manage everything in my head I now found myself having to verbalise or provide written reports on problems or ideas at the meetings and accept being questioned on them. There were times when I was gently nudged out of my comfort zone, but I knew that this was essential

"The Runner"

medicine for me and WA. This was management by imposition, and I would just have to get used to it.

Over the following meetings, the CRB would pore over key metrics. There is a saying in engineering that what gets measured gets done, and by measuring or quantifying the key metrics we could decide on which ones needed improving and then agree on actions to achieve improvements. It would take several meetings before the CRB would start to get an understanding of WA, its people, its technology, its customers and its suppliers, but that knowledge was being acquired steadily.

Prior to the establishment of the CRB, most activity at WA seemed to occur within the company, e.g., production, operations, R & D etc, but within a matter of months there was a hive of activity at management level that hadn't existed before. An early recommendation from the CRB was to recruit an Operations Manager. I had toyed around with this idea on several occasions, only to put it on the long finger, but the CRB felt that there was an urgent need to make this appointment. I duly advertised for and recruited an Operations Manager who would not only manage the Operations function but provide me with regular written reports so that I could keep abreast of what was going on in that area.

The next task was to recruit more engineers and to stop doing design work myself. I found that very difficult because of my love for designing electronic circuits, but I knew that I had to let go of that activity and entrust it to others. I recruited two engineers and trained them in RCD technology. The engineers worked well together and I was surprised that I could trust them to get on with their work. I told them that it was very important to enjoy moments of success whenever they completed a difficult project or task – to bask in that moment, just as I had done all those years earlier with the teleprinter.

"The Runner"

Improvements in performance could be seen in 1997 and WA would go on to make an operating profit in every subsequent year, thanks in large part to the role played by the CRB.

In October 1997 I had to attend an IEC meeting in Milan. It was unexpectedly cold in Milan on that occasion and when I checked into my hotel I found the room to be very cold. I tried adjusting the radiators but no heat emerged so I called reception to ask them to turn on the heat in my room. The receptionist explained that it was still October and that the heating would not be turned on until November in keeping with their standard practice.
I needed to work on some documents in preparation for the meeting the following day, but the room was uncomfortably cold. I then hit on an idea and searched the wardrobe and drawers until I found a hair dryer. Hair dryers will only produce heat while the switch is held in place so I locked the switch into the ON position with my shoelace and soon brought the room to a comfortable temperature.

I probably had the most comfortable room in the hotel that evening.

IEC and Cenelec started to impose more stringent technical requirements on RCDs, but fortunately due to my participation in those international bodies I was well aware of the new requirements and WA was able to upgrade its products in a timely manner to meet them.

In 1999 I was surprised to receive a phone call from the technical director of our former customer MEM. He informed me that MEM had just discovered a major problem with their inhouse designed RCD and he wanted to know if WA would be willing to supply them again. I was happy to jump at the opportunity, but I first wanted to know the nature of the problem.

"The Runner"

He explained that MEM had won a major contract in Australia for the supply of RCDs to the Olympic village being built in Sydney for the 2000 Olympic Games, and the problem was that their RCDs were tripping when someone operating a Walkie-Talkie came near them. The RCDs were tripping because of a high frequency signal being emitted by the Walkie-Talkie and he wanted to know if our RCDs were immune to such emissions.

I was pretty sure that our RCD technology would not be affected by Walkie-Talkies, but I sent him a few samples to ship out to Sydney for testing. Fortunately, they passed the test and WA was asked to gear up again for production of the MEM RCDs to be installed in the Olympic village.

I watched the opening ceremony on TV with some trepidation. The finale of the opening ceremony was to be the lighting of the Olympic flame by Cathy Freeman, the 400 metres sprinter.

She lit the flame on a large ring at ground level and the ring was then electronically taken very slowly up a ramp to the top of a tower where the Olympic flame would rest throughout the games.

"The Runner"

My heart was in my mouth as the ring of fire seemed to take forever to move up the ramp and in my mind I was screaming at my RCDs: "Don't trip. Please don't trip. Please don't trip."
The ring of fire finally reached the top of the ramp and it was then fixed in place. My relief was palpable.

Stories about the MEM RCD problem circulated within the RCD industry and we secured several new customers as a result and WA continued to grow steadily. In 2002 we built a dedicated design centre and recruited more engineers. By now WA had become an established player in the RCD industry globally and was highly regarded for its technology and its service to customers.

Although WA had grown over recent years it was still relatively small by international standards. The term SME means Small and Medium Enterprises, and we were one of the small ones. Because of our small size we sometimes encountered problems where a larger company felt that we could be pushed around, but I was determined that WA was not going to be pushed around by anyone, as the following story demonstrates.

I was beginning to become a bit of a globetrotter with trips to more and more countries visiting customers or attending IEC meetings etc. On one of those trips I flew to Germany to visit Bender Co., and I flew with Aer Lingus on the flight home. The SARS epidemic was in full flow at that time and flight attendants had to make an announcement about it. The announcement started by referring to the full name - Severe Acute Respiratory Syndrome, and warned that passengers with any of the respiratory symptoms were to report to immigration on landing in Dublin.

After the flight attendant had read out the statement a male German passenger sitting next to me said that he had a query and asked if I could help him. The conversation went something along the following lines.

"The Runner"

German Passenger: "Excuse me sir, but are you Irish?

Pat: "Yes".

German Passenger: "Well I speak English fairly well but I don't understand the difference between Severe and Acute. Could you explain that to me please."

Pat: "Well actually, there is no difference, but if they didn't include the word Severe the stewardess would have had to make an announcement about the ARS virus!"

Passenger: "Oh, I see. Thank you sir."
WA continued on an upward trajectory over the next few years and I started to add to the management team which enabled me to reduce my workload.

I began to reflect on myself and my wellbeing and I gave thought to a problem that had been an abiding burden since childhood. The problem was **Anger.**

It could be argued that I had a tough start in life, but so did lots of people from my childhood era. For many years after leaving school I found myself getting angry very quickly. Something would happen to trigger the powerful emotion of anger. I was never physically angry with people and so this was more a bottled-up type of anger. I assumed it had a lot to do with my childhood, and compounded by the stress of running my business, and to that extent I could almost justify those feelings. However, this was an emotional burden that I wished I could be rid of. At various stages in my life I went for counselling, first in England and later in Ireland to seek help to deal with the problem. Most counsellors would take me on a very painful journey back through my childhood and most of those sessions amounted to tear filled emotional torture that were totally unproductive. However, I went to see a lady counsellor in Galway around 2010, and after

"The Runner"

a couple of tear-filled sessions she said something to me that had a huge impact on my life, something that I wished I had heard many years sooner.

She simply said:

"Pat, you may not realise this but getting angry is an option. When you feel that emotion being triggered you can choose in that moment to allow the anger to engulf you or you can quite simply choose not to get angry. The choice is yours."

It was as if a mental switch that had been permanently ON could be turned OFF at my behest. I had never thought of anger as being an option, a choice that I could make. Instead of focusing on an event that could trigger anger and allow it to become an unstoppable driving force I could choose not to get angry. That session enabled me to turn the anger switch to OFF and shed the associated burden that I had carried with me for some sixty years. I have rarely been angry since that day, and I am indebted to that wonderful lady for her words of wisdom.

I had been single for a couple of years and feeling lonely and my vulnerability enticed me to enter a distance relationship in 2015. The initial euphoria led me to believe that my life had taken a turn for the better.

I continued to do my IEC work which involved a lot of international travel. My two best friends in IEC were Malcolm Mullins from the UK and Herman Vlutters from the Netherlands. We always teamed up and went out to dinner together and had a few beers on the evenings of those meetings. In 2017 Herman announced that he would retire from Standards work at the IEC meeting in Barcelona later that year. I was very sad at this news, and I was not looking forward to Herman's farewell meeting.

"The Runner"

A few days before the Barcelona meeting I discovered that my girlfriend had been cheating on me. Like "Humpty Dumpty", our relationship was broken and could not be put back together again, and I ended it. I was totally gutted and found myself grieving at my loss, but I had to somehow pull myself together and travel to Barcelona to say farewell to Herman. When I arrived at my hotel in Barcelona I checked in and then went to the bar to join some British and American colleagues. They soon noticed that I was not my usual self and they asked me what was wrong. I told them the story about my girlfriend, and they commiserated with me. Malcolm immediately offered to get me a beer to drown my sorrows.

We arrived just before the start of the conference the following morning and when Herman heard about my story he dashed over to give me a hug and offer his commiserations.

At the end of the meeting, the chairman announced that we would be having a special dinner at 7.00pm that evening at a local restaurant to bid farewell to Herman. He also said that several of the delegates would be accompanied by their wives or partners.

Malcolm always liked to have a couple of beers before such dinners and he persuaded me to join him at the bar in the hotel. In a genuine attempt to console me Malcolm kept raising the topic of my now ex-girlfriend, but he was driving me into a deeper and deeper sense of despair so I had to ask him to drop the subject. We left the hotel at about 6.45pm, and to my horror I discovered that Malcolm didn't have a clue where the restaurant was, and neither did I. We vaguely remembered the name, or part of it and we started asking for directions. Having no Spanish between us didn't help, but finally we met someone who knew where the restaurant was and gave us directions. We arrived there at about 7.15pm and discovered that everyone was seated at tables all around the room waiting patiently for us to arrive.

"The Runner"

Herman's wife Agneth was there, and the whole scene was funereal and surreal with glum faces everywhere.

Malcolm and I looked around the room for a table to sit at, but the only vacant table was a small one in the middle of the room. With great embarrassment we took our seats like two errant schoolboys who were being humiliated in front of the whole class. The dinner was a painfully slow sober affair, presumably because everyone was anticipating the moment of sadness that was to follow with the public adieu to Herman. Malcolm decided to dash out to the toilet just as the chairman rose to prepare himself for his farewell speech to Herman. He recounted the many years that they had worked together and the valuable contribution that Herman had made in IEC over the previous thirty years.
I was already in a sad emotional state because of my recent breakup, but the chairman's words about Herman were bringing me closer to a tipping point. I had managed to avoid eye contact with Herman throughout the speech because I was afraid that I would be overcome with emotion and start crying, but at the moment that the chairman asked Herman to come up and receive his award I looked over at Herman and saw him wipe a tear from his eye. As Herman rose to go to the top table the dam burst, and I knew in that moment that nothing was going to hold back my oncoming torrent of tears. Herman thanked the Chairman and the members and that was followed by a resounding round of applause. I couldn't applaud because I was too busy wiping tears from my eyes.

Agneth noticed my state and immediately shouted:

"Oh my God, Pat's crying."

She then rushed over to console me. Several other women rushed over to console me and suddenly I was surrounded by comforting women. I tried to blurt out that I wasn't crying because of

"The Runner"

Herman, but no one was listening. Just then Malcolm returned from his long sojourn in the toilet and saw all these women consoling me and he realised that I was in a bad emotional state. Next thing he blurted out:

"Jesus Pat, that bitch really broke your heart."

One of the women turned on Malcolm and said:

"How dare you call Herman a bitch!!

Malcolm was shocked and retorted:
"I didn't call Herman a bitch!!"

But the situation was now out of hand with Malcolm hopelessly trying to explain himself. The women abandoned me and started to vent their anger on Malcolm who was having great difficulty explaining himself. As I looked through the melee of women I could see Herman wiping tears from his eyes, but no one was paying any attention to him because of the exchanges between Malcolm and the angry women.

Herman and I met up with Malcolm the following morning and I had to explain to them both what had really transpired. Malcolm was shocked at the notion that anyone would think he had referred to Herman as "that bitch", but by then we could laugh at the whole episode.

WA was now an internationally trading company and subject to more intense competition, but it was also starting to come to the attention of potential buyers. One such company was TRC, and they invited me to Florida to meet with them. I wasn't particularly interested in selling WA at that time, but I was also not impressed by them and I felt that they were not a good fit for WA.

"The Runner"

The trip wasn't a complete waste of time because I had allowed myself a few extra days to play some golf. On my final day I went to a golf shop to buy a ball collector like the one shown below.

The subsequent conversation went as follows.

Pat to shop assistant: "Hi, I'm looking for a ball collector. It has a bag that can hold about 50 golf balls."

"The Runner"

What Lies Beneath

In his book: "The Moon's a Balloon", David Niven mentioned that when the garden is at its rosiest, that's when the weeds are at their busiest. In effect he was saying that the rosy state will not be sustained if we ignore the weeds taking root.

Thanks largely to the CRB and the performance of the new management team, WA seemed to be doing quite well, and viewing the accounts for any one recent year alone would reinforce that viewpoint. However, when I reviewed the accounts for several recent years I spotted something that had largely gone unnoticed. Charts 4 and 5 show Sales and Operating Profits for the years 2009 to 2016.

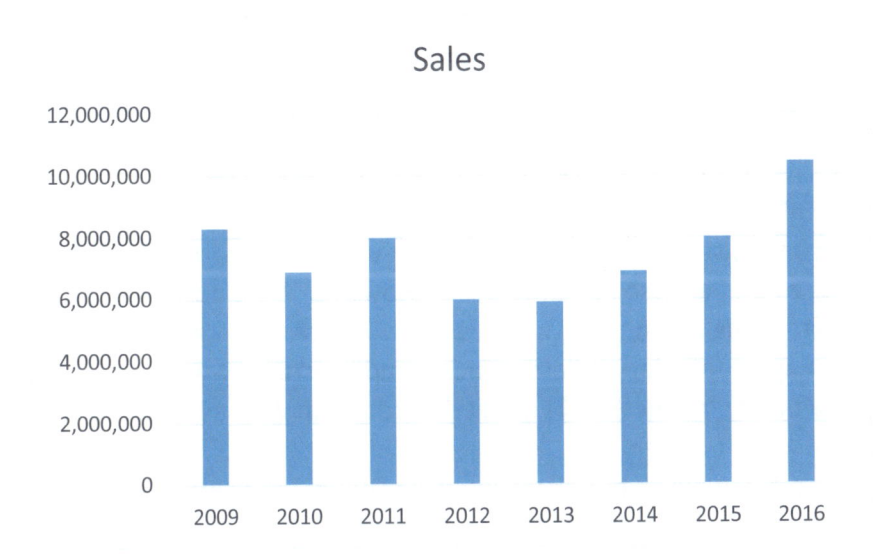

Chart 4 – Sales

"The Runner"

Operating Profit

Chart 5 – Operating Profit

The good news was that sales were increasing. The bad news was that there was an ongoing erosion in operating profits. This was partly due to the financial crisis but also due to competitive pressures which were forcing WA to reduce or maintain prices against a backdrop of rising costs, and this was impacting on profit margins. Most companies will suffer from a drop in profitability at various stages and in many cases it will be self-correcting, e.g. by an increase in demand, etc. However if the downward trend is sustained there will be a growing risk of failure. It is management's job to detect such trends and deal with them in a timely manner, and I needed to come up with a solution.

I was driving back to Ballinasloe from Dublin airport one evening in late 2016 when I pulled up at a set of traffic lights which had just gone from amber to red. They eventually turned to green, but during that pause I came up with an idea for pricing our products which I called the traffic lights system.

I decided that we would place all products into three categories, Red, Yellow and Green, based on their gross profit margin.

"The Runner"

Green = A gross Profit Margin > 45%

Amber = A gross Profit Margin 35 – 45%

Red = A gross Profit Margin <35%

Note that Green is at the top in my traffic light because that is the prime target for profitability. I decided that during the course of 2017 we would drastically reduce the number of Red products by increasing their prices or discontinuing those products by the end of that year. At that stage about 35% of our products were in the Red zone, about 50% in the Amber zone and the remainder in the Green zone. I reasoned that the Red zone products were using up valuable resources with minimal contribution to profits. In effect, they were acting as deadweight on the company's performance. Customers were informed that those products would have to undergo a price increase of 10% or be discontinued by year end. In effect I was willing to let go of low margin products and allow our competitors to have that business. Surprisingly a majority of customers agreed to the price increase, some negotiated a lower price increase, and the remaining products were discontinued. This had the effect of reducing the Red zone to about 15% of products by the end of 2017. In parallel to that action, I notified customers with products in the Amber zone that we would apply a 5% price increase on all future orders, and I waited for the pushback. There was surprisingly little pushback so by year end the Green zone had increased from about 15% to about 30% of sales.

When the Red zone finally reached about 5% of sales I moved the three bands up as follows.

"The Runner"

Green = A gross Profit Margin > 55%

Amber = A gross Profit Margin 45 – 55%

Red = A gross Profit Margin <45%

This had the desired effect of temporarily increasing the size of the RED zone to about 25% and thus motivating us to target more products for price increases or elimination. Over the following year several more products were eliminated from the Red zone and the others had their prices increased with the result that profits increased, but hugely importantly, valuable resources were freed up to facilitate development of new high margin products.

This policy to kill off Red zone products was continued in all subsequent years and the effect on profitability was huge. The combined effects are reflected in the following charts for Sales and Operating profits.

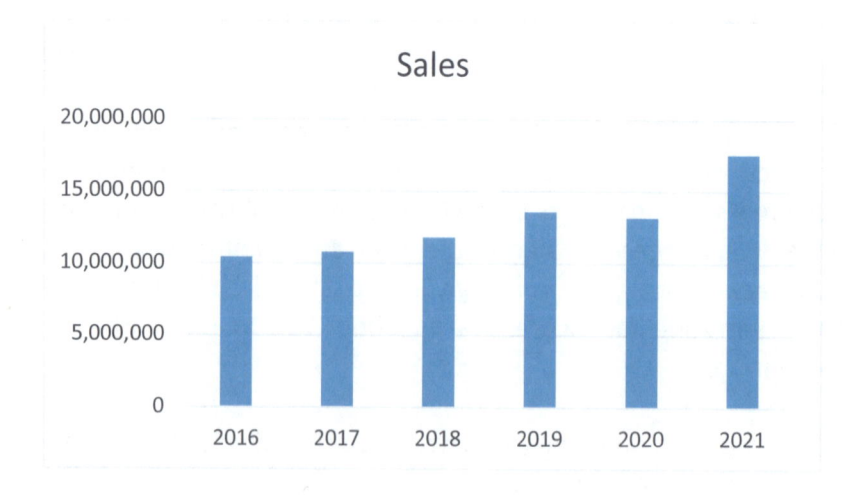

Chart 6 – Sales

"The Runner"

Operating Profits

2016	~500,000
2017	~600,000
2018	~2,000,000
2019	~2,800,000
2020	~3,200,000
2021	~7,000,000

Chart 7 – Operating Profits

Journey's End

In 2022 I decided that it was time to sell WA. A prospectus was prepared by DAVY stockbrokers in Dublin and sent out to potential buyers around the world. We received a total of 27 expressions of interest initially and we had to go through them to decide who to engage further with.

WA had a total of 45 Employees at that time with 9 based in Spain, 2 in the UK and the remainder at the Ballinasloe site. Employees had been very loyal to WA through good times and bad. Whilst most employees had been with WA for at least ten years six employees had been with the company for over 30 years. I wanted to repay that loyalty by ensuring that WA was not sold to an asset stripper, so I sought out new owners who would retain the current operations in Ireland, UK and Spain. I found a suitable buyer and WA was sold in February 2023 to a USA multinational company after 38 years under my stewardship.

"The Runner"

It is interesting to note that WA came about because of a USA multinational company, Square D, and its future has been assured by another USA multinational company.

No Simple Explanation

On 17 August 1963 I boarded a ship bound for Liverpool. I was a scrawny 16-year-old with nothing more than the clothes I wore. I didn't even have a penny in my pocket that day. In 2023 I sold my company for a large sum of money. I don't have a simple explanation for that transition but as I reflect on the intervening years I can identify some factors that may have contributed to it.

A chance viewing of a speech by Harold Wilson in 1965 planted in my head the notion of becoming an electronics engineer.

A chance viewing of an advert by the Royal Navy added to that notion and enticed me to join up and try to become an electronics engineer.

A chance viewing of an advert by Square D Company in a UK magazine that resulted in me coming back to Ireland.

Those fortuitous events led to the launch of Western Automation. The training and the experiences I gained in the Royal Navy transformed me into a competent and capable person, and gave me a belief that if I applied myself I could start and run a business successfully. The subsequent success of WA is testimony to that.

In my school years I always strove to be the best I could be at whatever I did, be it academic or sport related. That desire seemed to pull me forward day by day and on through my life. There were no big achievements along the way but each small success added to previous successes and gave me confidence and belief that almost any obstacle could be overcome by commitment to the task at hand and sheer determination.

"The Runner"

As far back as I can remember I felt a need to excel, as reflected in the mantra that I introduced in WA:

"Good enough is not good enough. Good enough is for others. We can do better."

Maybe it mostly boils down to that simple principle.

"The Runner"

Chapter 4 – The Gift of Family and Friends

I am the product of my mother and an unknown father. I came from a different production line from my older siblings, but my life and that of Dennis, Pearl, Ethel and Val were intertwined regardless. Call it fate or whatever, but they brought love and a richness to my life that might not otherwise have existed.

It is regrettable that none of us ever felt a similar bond with our younger brother Anthony. He was raised by the Commins family. He had little or no bond to our mother and rarely referred to her and he never visited her when she was sent to St. Brigid's asylum. Anthony moved to London in the late 1960's. I only met him once as an adult, in 1969. I was disappointed when he referred to Mrs Commins as his mam, but I understood and accepted how that came about. Anthony was working on a building site in London in 1975 when he fell through an asbestos roof and died shortly afterwards. He was aged 26.

I stayed in close contact with Val, Ethel, Pearl and Dennis throughout their lives. Pearl is currently a sprightly 83 years old. She never remarried because she always said that no one could ever replace Leo.

Dennis and Pat had eight children initially and Dennis decided that enough was enough and that Pat would have to go on the pill. Four years later Pat became pregnant again. Dennis told me that he was shocked but that he would just have to accept another child into the family. I told him to think of it as a P.S. – a postscript.

Dennis turned to me and said: "P.S. That's an interesting way to look at it."

Several months later Pat gave birth to a boy. Dennis named him "Peter Simon" !

"The Runner"

Dennis had been very healthy all his life but in 2018 he got a bad dose of the flu and became seriously ill. He died later that year and is buried in Rugeley.

Ethel married and had three daughters initially. That marriage ended in divorce, but she remarried and had another daughter. Ethel was a lifelong heavy smoker and she died of breathing complications in 2020. I couldn't attend the funeral because of travel restrictions imposed during the Covid lockdown. Ethel was cremated and her daughters kindly agreed to allow her ashes to be brought to Galway so that they could be sprinkled on the sea in Galway Bay. When the travel restrictions were lifted Val brought her ashes to Galway and he and Pearl and I went out to Silver Strand for our quiet ceremony. Val took off his shoes and socks and rolled up his trousers and waded into the water. We bade goodbye to Ethel as Val sprinkled her ashes on the water. It was an extremely emotional event.

One day I was looking out at the Bay and watching the cascading waves come to shore. I imagined that Ethel was riding the waves and suddenly a poem just seemed to flow into my head. I wrote down the words quickly to capture them. Here they are.

Ethel Marie
We sprinkled the ashes of Ethel Marie
On Galway Bay's Atlantic sea
She rode the tide from Galway Bay
To Neverland, far away
And then returned the very next day
To her beloved Galway Bay
Seagulls screeched as if to say
"Ethel Marie is on her way"
No day goes by that I don't see
From my window – Ethel Marie.

"The Runner"

Val married Marion in 1971 and they had three daughters, Michelle, Mariessa and Claire. Although I lived in Ireland from 1979, Val and I remained very close, visiting each other several times most years. To non-family eyes we were like chalk and cheese but we had a bond that left them bemused and us amused. The bond established in childhood remained with us throughout our adult lives.

Sadly, Val was diagnosed with a form of bone cancer in 2020. The initial treatments kept it at bay for two years but he started to become seriously ill in late December 2022 and was hospitalised. He recovered sufficiently to go home in January, and in February 2023 I managed to fly Val and family members to Galway to raise his spirits, but we felt that this was likely to be his last trip to Galway. We were surprised at how energetic and rejuvenated he seemed to be on that visit, and it certainly lifted his spirits. His health fluctuated wildly over the following weeks and he was admitted to a hospice. I visited Val several times over the following months and he became excited at the notion of the book being finished so that he could read it. I mentioned to him that as I was writing Chapter I recounted how we used to play cowboys and I started to say:
"Get off your horse ..."

But before I could finish it Val excitedly interrupted with:
"...and drink your milk."

We laughed at how both of us could recall that role play.

Sadly his condition deteriorated over the following months. The four girls in his life gave him as much care and attention as possible during this sad period.

I managed to visit him several times during those months and I found those visits becoming increasingly emotional, especially the last one. The hospice had informed us that Val had just days to

"The Runner"

live. I brought Pearl over to join me when I knew that this would be our final chance to say goodbye.

Val recognised us but he was struggling to speak at that stage. I sat on the edge of the bed and held his hand. He tried to speak but I told him to rest. I watched him drift off to sleep. The time came for Pearl and me to leave for the airport to catch our return flight home. I kissed Val on the forehead and said goodbye. Pearl did likewise. My face was awash with tears as we made our way out of the room. His daughters took over comforting him. Pearl and I caught the flight to Dublin. The following morning I received the news that Val had passed away peacefully during the night. I had lost my wonderful brother.

Val was cremated and his family kindly agreed to bring his ashes to Galway. Twenty-four family members came to Silver Strand for the event. Claire had brought the container of the ashes and handed it to me. My daughter Kerry had brought a bunch of yellow roses, and these were handed out to the family members. Claire and Michelle accompanied me as I waded into the water to knee high. I then slowly sprinkled the ashes on the lapping waves and the ebbing tide carried them out to sea. The other family members tossed the yellow rose petals on to the waves at the shoreline and the waves collected the petals to form them into a yellow flotilla that escorted Val on out through the bay into the open sea.

Just two years earlier, Val and I had performed a similar ceremony with Ethel's ashes and he had now joined with Ethel in Galway Bay. I look forward to them both coming back into Galway Bay each day to say hello to me. One day I will join them.

A Fun Guy
Whenever Val and I got together the resultant energy could light up a room. We shared a wonderful sense of humour that often left other people somewhat bewildered. Val could get very loud

"The Runner"

and excitable when he had a few drinks, so much so that we were thrown out of pubs on several occasions.

Val and I would often go to the Kings Arms pub in Sandy for a drink and a chat, and sometimes we would play a game of dominoes against some other guys. Val and I were a formidable pair and we won quite often. However, Val had a problem in that sometimes when we won and he had had a lot to drink he would lose the run of himself and start to gloat over our opponents. One night he went too far and as our two opponents got up to leave the table one of them said:

"Right, we've had enough of you two. Finish your drinks and we'll be waiting out back for you."

Suddenly the atmosphere went chillingly cold. The landlord knew that this was trouble, but he was helpless to stop it. When the two guys went out to the back yard I decided to try to make light of the situation. I stood up and did an Oliver Hardy impression:

"Well, this is another fine mess you've gotten us into", but Val wasn't amused. This was serious and I began to recall the incident in Lichfield cathedral when I was invited to "step outside".
I couldn't act dumb this time. After a momentary pause Val stood up and said:

"Right. Finish your drink."

We both finished our drinks, braced ourselves – and then dashed out the front door and laughed hysterically as we ran all the way back to Val's house with visions of the two guys at the back of the pub shadow boxing.

Val could never keep a secret when he had some good news. When I was travelling over to visit him in March 2023 I called him and asked him to record the Manchester United v Nottingham

"The Runner"

Forest match so that I could watch it later at his house. Val knew that I was a keen Man Utd fan, so I had to tell him loud and clear not to tell me the score. He greeted me when I arrived at the house and said that he had recorded the match, and as I sat down to watch it he said:

"Now, I know you don't want me to tell you the score so I'm not going to tell you, but you'll be very happy with the result!!

All I could say was: "Ah, for God's sakes, Val", but he insisted that he hadn't told me the score!!

Val

I think about Val most days since his passing and I am reminded of him every time I look at the sea in Galway Bay and recall the sprinkling of his ashes on the ebbing tide at Silver Strand. One day

"The Runner"

in late October I took a stroll along the Prom and as usual I thought about Val. It was a beautiful sunny day, a feel good and uplifting sort of day. When I got home I reflected on the walk along the Prom and the following words came to me.

Remembering Val
I stand on the Prom and gaze across the bay
On a beautiful October's day
There's lots of talk and lots of smiles
As people clock up the miles
The sun is shining, the sea is glistening
There's noise all around but I'm not listening
My thoughts drift slowly out to sea
On top of waves that set them free
I think of Val somewhere out there
And selfishly wish he was here
I then realise that he is here
Here, there, and everywhere
Ashes scattered on the sea
That was how we set him free
To bring joy far and wide
On each and every surging tide
The sun bathes me in gentle heat
As the sea makes its retreat
I must let go of my best friend
There are others he must tend
But he'll be back very soon
His smile reflected in the moon
Tomorrow brings another day
For me to stroll in Galway Bay
And think of all the joy we shared
Blessed was I that we were paired.

"Paired" refers to how we were paired off as children to be sent to Letterfrack and then on to St. Joseph's.

"The Runner"

Coming Home
I didn't realise it at the time, but in taking up the job offer and moving to Ballinasloe in October 1979 I had started on a new journey that would eventually take me back to Galway.

By 2010 Paul and Kerry had long grown up and left home to start their own families and I started to think about possibly moving to Galway city in anticipation of retirement. House prices had fallen because of the economic setbacks of 2008 to 2010 so I was able to buy an old bungalow in Salthill at a reasonable price. I had it demolished and replaced with a two-storey house with a beautiful view of Galway Bay. I felt that I had returned to my spiritual home almost 60 years after leaving it and I looked forward to my new life in Galway. However, my wife and I had grown apart and our marriage ended in separation in 2013 followed later by a divorce.

I started taking regular walks along the Prom all the way to Claddagh Hall and memories came flooding back as I passed the site of the former location of St. Joseph's school. I suppressed the negative memories as much as possible and gave prominence to my positive experiences there.

I recalled the day that Val and I arrived at St. Joseph's in 1954 and my first encounter with Dennis. I recalled the sad encounter with my mother. I remembered catching the mackerel and having it served up to me on a beautiful dish. I reminisced about the Sunday walks and about becoming "The Runner" and how exhilarated I was.

When I walked towards Blackrock and then on past Galway golf club I remembered seeing the men with "sticks" crossing the road to go into a "field".

Throughout my school years in Salthill I never had any silly notions that one day I might become a member of Galway Golf Club, but we now lived in the 21st century and times had changed and I

"The Runner"

could at least aspire to become a member, even if not accepted. In 2013 I applied to become a member of Galway Golf club and I waited anxiously for a reply. A few weeks later I got a phone call inviting me to meet the club manager, Padraic Fahy. I subsequently met with Padraic and we chatted about my moving back to Galway. He told me my application had been accepted and he welcomed me to the club.

As I stood up to leave, Padraic shook hands with me and said: "Pat, you have just joined one of the friendliest golf clubs in Ireland. My advice to you is to get out there and start playing golf and meet the members."
I thanked Padraic, and as I made my way home I was both emotional and euphoric. I had become a member of Galway Golf Club. "The Runner" had become a member of Galway Golf Club. Who would have believed it. I called Val that evening and he was delighted for me.

The following evening I decided to take up Padraic's advice and I went down to the first tee at about 7.00pm. There was a guy standing on the first tee and about to tee off, so I decided to let him tee off before saying anything. He hit a nice tee shot and I was duly impressed and I said:

"Great shot. Do you mind if I join you?"

He replied: "Yes I do", and he headed off down the first fairway and left me flabbergasted.

As I started to recall Padraic's words about this being one of the friendliest golf clubs in Ireland I couldn't help but think that there must be some dreadful golf clubs out there, and wasn't I lucky not to have joined one of them!!

I played a few holes on my own and then went into the bar to have a "friendly" pint, and I was pleasantly surprised when I was made welcome by some of the other members. I told them about my experience on the first tee and that story went viral.

A Golfing Interview
My Sunday ritual for many years had been to play golf with a fourball group in Ballinasloe, but I didn't know anyone in Galway golf club so each Sunday I would just put my name on a line where there was a space and go out with total strangers. I would play with different people each week depending on where I could find a spot to add my name. Most golfers like to get into a regular fourball group, and I knew it would take me time to get to know people and indeed for them to get to know me.

One Sunday I put my name on a line with three other guys, Tom, John and Pat. We had the usual introductions on the first tee, and it was obvious that these guys played together regularly. However, their usual fourth partner was missing and hence my meeting this group. We started playing and when we got to the fourth tee I pulled my drive down the left side of the fairway and so did Tom, so Tom and I walked slowly towards our balls. Tom was somewhat curious about me and said:

"So what's your story, Pat?"

I told him that I had moved to Galway the previous year and that I was fortunate to be able to join Galway GC. He asked me about my family, and I told him that I had recently separated. He offered his commiserations and then said:

"Don't worry, Pat. I've been there. You'll find someone else."

I wasn't too sure about that, but I thanked him for his comments. A similar thing happened on the 7th hole when I found myself heading towards the trees on the right side of the fairway with John. He was somewhat curious about me and said:

"The Runner"

"So what's your story, Pat?"

I told him that I had moved to Galway the previous year and that I was fortunate to be able to join Galway GC. He asked me about my family, and I told him that I had recently separated. He offered his commiserations and then said:

"Don't worry, Pat. I've been there. You'll find someone else."

I said: "Thanks John. That's very kind of you."
The 12th hole is a long and expansive par 5 and I sliced my drive, and it shot way off down a slope on the right side of the fairway. Pat did the same thing, but Tom and John were in the middle of the fairway. Pat and I went down the slope and played our second shots and it was a long walk back up to the fairway. As Pat strolled alongside me he said:

"So, what's your story, Pat?"

I told him that I had moved to Galway the previous year and that I was fortunate to be able to join Galway GC. He asked me about my family, and I told him that I had recently separated. He offered his commiserations and then said:

"Don't worry, Pat. I've been there. You'll find someone else."

I said: "Thank Pat. That's very kind of you."

At this stage I was beginning to wonder if this was some sort of a setup, but it turned out that all of these guys had genuinely gone through separations. When the round finished the guys invited me into the clubhouse for a drink. As we were about to leave the clubhouse Tom asked me if I had my own regular fourball group. I said no and that I would just put my name down on a line at random the following Sunday as usual. Tom said, "Don't bother. John will put you on our line." He then explained that their previous group member was no longer playing golf and that's how a "vacancy" in their group arose.

Golf is a great social sport and I have been fortunate to play with some wonderful people over the years. Sadly some have passed away. I currently play mostly with a regular group of golfers, John Rabbitt, Pat Holland, Pat Ivers, Tom Callinan and Barry Cunningham. No one will ever know the excruciating pain they have endured over several years as they watched me butcher Galway golf course. Their patience would have tested St. Job as they watched me week in and week out traverse every blade of grass and every grain of sand on that course. There's nowhere on that course that I haven't traversed, with the exception of water. On many occasions they volunteered to join me in my search for golf balls just so that they too could get more acquainted with areas of Galway golf course previously unknown to them. I cannot imagine anyone else bearing up under such duress for so long were it not for the fact that I paid them weekly for accompanying me on my outings. They always assured me that they took the money with the utmost reluctance, but I had my doubts. However, in recent years most of them have been brought down to my level of mediocrity which has finally enabled me to not only choke off the cash spigot but generate a small cash flow in my direction. I, of course, take their money with the utmost reluctance. After all, golf is an honourable game played by gentlemen.

I also joined Galway Bridge Club on St. Mary's Road and thanks to the golf club and the bridge club I met a lot of people and made new friends, all of which gave me a wonderful sense of belonging and that I was finally home.

People
I have been very fortunate to have had some wonderful people in my life, people who didn't care about where I came from. I would

"The Runner"

not have achieved half of what I did achieve without their encouragement and support.

I returned to Galway after a 50-year absence and I didn't know anyone there at that time. I gradually met some nice people and made new friends who helped me through the difficult period of my divorce, but also in making me feel at home in Galway.

After I sold WA, I arranged to bring a group of fellow golfers to Dromoland Castle for a mini golf event with an overnight stay. Here is a photo of the group taken in the cocktail lounge of Dromoland Castle.

From left to right:
Michael Lawler, Pat McGann, Pat Ivers, Ted Murphy, John Rabbitt, Barry Cunningham, Pat Ward, Kevin O'Reilly, Martin O'Neill, Peter Whelan, Noel Ivers, Tom Callanan.

"The Runner"

Reflections On a Life
I now have the benefit of looking back on my life, a life that had a difficult and a traumatic start. A childhood where insecurity and uncertainty formed its shaky foundation. A childhood spent in the confines of Letterfrack and St. Joseph's. A childhood of male dominance where control was achieved through fear. A childhood where social skills were limited to the regimen of the institution and left me totally ill equipped to cope with the world outside those confines - the real world.

In my poem, The Sunday Walk, I wrote the lines:

*"The outside world is not for real
To us that world holds no appeal"*

That was untrue, but in thinking those thoughts I could learn to cope in my world. The outside world was certainly the world I craved for, but a world that I had minimal exposure to and little understanding of. I was shocked when I left St. Joseph's and discovered how ill equipped I was to cope in that world. I was fortunate that I had the ability to gradually make sense of it and over time I learned to adapt and become comfortable in it.

Sometimes I think of life as being like the game of bridge. You may not like the hand you have been dealt and understandably wish you had been dealt a better one, but you have no option but to play the one you were dealt. With a positive attitude you may surprise yourself at how much more you can get out of it than first expected. I certainly was.

Ireland
Thankfully the country that demonised single mothers and incarcerated their children is no more. There is no such thing as an "illegitimate" child in Ireland anymore. The suffocating

influence of the Catholic Church is no more. There is a wonderful sense of freedom and optimism in Ireland today.

In previous years, I and many others looked to the USA as the land of opportunity, but I firmly believe that Ireland now has that appeal in abundance, and having visited about fifty countries, I honestly believe there is no better country in the world.

The Power of Education
Education played a huge part in my life and in many ways it provided me with a stairway to personal development and achievement. It started when Brother Egan decided to give me two more years of education rather than put me to work on the school farm. The educational options and facilities in the Royal Navy took me further than my wildest dreams. Undertaking a Diploma in Professional Management with the Open University changed my approach to running my business. This was taken to another level with my MSc in Management Practice with Trinity/IMI.

I am currently studying for a Doctorate in Business Administration with Warwick Business School. My research topic and my thesis will be based on business failure. I hope to use my doctorate to enable me to work with firms to identify factors that raise their risk of failure and help them to mitigate those risks.

Confidence & Self-Belief
To write this book I had to start by transporting myself back to the 3-year-old me, a pitiful boy clinging to his 5-year-old brother and crying out for his mother. That boy had to grow up and stop clinging and crying. Letting go requires a belief that in doing so life will get better.

My achievements in the Royal Navy gave me a confidence and a self-belief that had been totally lacking theretofore. It was the RN

"The Runner"

that taught me to view most failures as temporary setbacks on the road to success.

A Haunting Melody
"Whispering Hope" is the name of a hymn that we learned in school. Here are the lyrics.

> Soft as the voice of an angel
> Breathing a lesson unheard
> Hope with a gentle persuasion
> Whispers her comforting word
> Wait 'til the darkness is over
> Wait 'til the tempest is done
> Hope for the sunshine tomorrow
> After the darkness is gone.

I often thought about those words in moments when I was feeling low - in St. Joseph's, in my early days in England, and in subsequent times of sadness. I sometimes felt that they helped to lift me up and give me the strength to journey on. I am now in my twilight years and I have time to reflect on that hymn without a sense of sadness or feeling forlorn, and I have found myself wondering about the words:

> "Hope with a gentle persuasion
> Whispers her comforting word"

I find it intriguing that the writer of that hymn referred to Hope as "her". Could it be that "Hope" was my mother whispering to me, coaxing me along on my journey. I'd like to think so.

Please go to this link to enjoy it at as a song:
Daniel O'Donnell & Mary Duff - Whispering Hope,
www.youtube.com/watch?v=sqK4lu17gpl

"The Runner"

And here is a link to a beautiful Irish version of the song that I highly recommend viewing.

Whispering Hope by the Presentation School Choir, Kilkenny, www.youtube.com/watch?v=dcnkvRAK9CQ

Three Major Decisions
As I look back on my life I can identify three pivotal decisions that proved to be very fortuitous and rewarding. The first was to join the Royal Navy which gave me stability and a career. The second was to return to Ireland, which led to my setting up Western Automation. The third was my move back to Galway. Prior to coming back to Galway, I never had a sense of belonging, but I have it now. In 2018 I was asked to give a city tour to two American American couples visiting Galway. I had to read up on the history of Galway so as to make the tour interesting and I was amazed at how much I learned about Galway in the process. In 2019 I was asked to give a city tour to five German ladies. In each case I found the tours very enjoyable, and I discovered that taking visitors on a city tour was a great way of increasing my knowledge of Galway, but also of reinforcing that sense of belonging.

Success
For some people success may be measured in money. For others it may be through achievements in sport or politics, etc.

For me success was having reconnected with Val, Ethel, Pearl and Dennis. It was having my own family which in turn gave me children and grandchildren. It was shedding my feelings of inferiority and replacing them with feelings of self-confidence.
It was achieving a sense of normality.

"The Runner"

Thank you for reading my story.

If you liked this book, please tell your friends. If you didn't like it, please say nothing and let that be our little secret.

Please feel free to contact me by email at:
therunner1947@gmail.com

Paperback copies and ebook copies are available at
www.therunner.ie and all Amazon webstores.

Paperback copies are also available at Charlie Byrne Bookstore at Middle Street, Galway, Ireland, and from their website:
www.charliebyrne.ie/product/the-runner

Please consider leaving a review at www.amazon.co.uk

Pat Ward

"The Runner"

Notes